Dwight Van de Vate, Jr., former president of
the Southern Society for Philosophy and
Psychology, has contributed to leading
philosophy journals. Since earning his B.A.
at Wesleyan and his Ph.D. at Yale he has
taught at Mississippi, Florida State, Memphis
State, and the University of Tennessee,
where he is professor of philosophy.

Romantic Love
A Philosophical Inquiry

In Wahrheit ist denn auch die inhaltliche Entfaltung der Philosophie von Schritt zu Schritt der doppelte Prozeß: das Wissen des Gegenstandes und das Wissen um das Wissen des Gegenstandes. Diese Doppelreihigkeit ist keine äußerliche, kein Nebeneinanderherlaufen von zweierlei Erkenntnis. Es ist durchaus ein einziger einheitlicher Duktus fortschreitenden Begreifens, in dem jedesmal das Begriffene auch ein Begreifen des Begriffes nach sich zieht und so den Gegenstand verschiebt; wodurch wiederum der Begriff sich verschiebt, verflüssigt, und über sich hinausschreitet.

—*Nicolai Hartmann,* Die Philosophie des deutschen Idealismus

Romantic Love
A Philosophical Inquiry

Dwight Van de Vate, Jr.

The Pennsylvania State University Press
University Park and London

Library of Congress Cataloging in Publication Data

Van de Vate, Dwight, 1929–
    Romantic love, a philosophical inquiry.

    Includes index.
    1. Love. I. Title.
BD436.V36   306.7   81–47171
ISBN 0–271–00288–3   AACR2

Designed by Dolly Carr

Printed in the United States of America

This book is dedicated
to my parents and my children.

Contents

Preface

About ten years ago, I began introducing students to philosophy by asking them how one might go about analyzing certain large, disputable abstractions. In different years, I used "the soul," "friendship," "madness," and "love." I chose those ideas because they seemed to me important and yet I had no idea what would count as a good analysis of any of them. Also, I suspected there was some connection between my sense of their importance and my inability to analyze them, though I could not say what that connection was. I felt puzzled and challenged, and I hoped my students might share those feelings.

This book began, then, as an introduction to philosophy, and I hope it may still serve as one. It is also a book about love. As a rule, writers about love start by taking for granted what sort of thing love is. Love is assumed to be psychological, religious, sociological, philosophical, or what-have-you. The features of the resulting analysis—the size of the problem, what evidence is relevant, the style of presentation and method of proof—are dictated by that initial assumption, which can only be a dogmatic assumption. Here, however, that initial assumption itself is our primary concern: this book is about love by first being about the question "What is love?" An analysis or explanation of romantic love does result, but as a byproduct of an analysis of what should count as explaining love. I regard second-order analysis, analysis of what should count as an analysis, as simply another name for philosophy.

Accordingly, the thin thread of consequentiality that ties the book together lies in its movement from one question to another. The detailed analyses of individual questions—all of them interpretations of "What is love?"—are less important. We begin where we are, with our layman's certainty that love is a feeling, but a feeling too intimate and mysterious to be defined, let alone explained. We conclude by explaining that certainty. Our main concern, however, is not to give this explanation but to justify it, to show why its principles of explanation are relevant to its explanandum.

Love is said to be an indefinable feeling. We put that indefinable feeling to work in definite ways, however, and the uses we make of it provide definite clues to what we really think it is. In Part I, we follow those clues. We find that the expression "the use we make of love" is ambiguous, for it might refer to what each of us individually does with love, or to what all of us collectively do with it. The former depends on the latter; in other words, individual loving feelings and actions owe their intelligibility to love as an institution, to our collective habit of supposing that such feelings exist and tend to dominate those who feel them.

In Part II, therefore, we analyze what the institution of romantic love contributes to all of us collectively, to "society." This analysis is "functionalistic" in the familiar sociological sense, and we are led to pose a familiar type of objection to it. When we do so, we discover that the idea of love's contribution to society can be no clearer than the idea of society itself, and so we ask what society is. The "society" of the social scientist is the counterpart of the "nature" of the natural scientist. Objects as vast as these make for vague explanations. Therefore we turn back to ourselves, to the activity of explaining which led us to ask what nature and society are, and in particular, to the objectivity which defines that activity. This objectivity is the subject of Part III, "Inquiry and the Inquirer." In the end, we shall see in what sense love is inexplicable and how the intimacies of love are related to the intimacies of explanation. In a concluding section, I summarize the conception of philosophy which motivates this inquiry into love, a conception that I hope will be found useful and appealing both in the closet world of academic philosophy and in the great world beyond.

By taking too long to write this book, I have accumulated too many debts to acknowledge as I would and should, especially to a large number of extraordinarily patient students. The University of Tennessee has supported my research activities over the years and helped support publication of this book. I am grateful on both counts. My colleagues here and elsewhere have tolerated me affectionately, and I thank them for that. Among the individuals who have been especially helpful are J. Austin, R. Edwards, J. Hanel, W. Herndon, B. Moser, G. Overton, M. Peterson, A. Ramos, S. Reaven, C. Reynolds, D. Scates, and N. Smith. The following read the entire manuscript and offered valuable encouragement: D. Browning, J. Davis, S. Eichler, T. Hood, and R. Sullivan. A book on love ought to register the author's personal feelings somewhere. This book does so in this paragraph and in the dedication.

Introduction
Constructing a Theory

The Science of Questions

One traditional way of defining philosophy is as the science of questions, that discipline which asks questions not about the world, but about questions themselves. Thus if we think of a *question* simply as whatever may occasion a difference of opinion, and of a *proof* or *explanation* as whatever will properly settle a question (the emphasis being on "properly"), then we may say that the *subject matter* of a *science* or *discipline* will be a set of related questions, and the proofs that will decide those questions will be the *theory* of that subject matter. Someone *expert* in a theory will be able to decide its questions with a proficiency superior to the layman's and satisfactory to his fellow experts. The *philosopher*, then, will be the expert on questions, that specialist who asks what are the different kinds of question and what sorts of proof will decide them.

This aporetic or question-oriented definition identifies philosophy with logic, broadly conceived. It has the advantage of providing a reply to the familiar criticism that philosophy is an idly speculative activity from which each special science separates itself as soon as that science matures, as soon as its experts have learned how to construct genuine proofs. The reply is that one function of philosophy is to bring about this very result. We humans have the habit of asking ourselves large, vague, threatening questions, questions which seem neither answerable nor avoidable. Sometimes these questions can be made more manageable, can be transformed into well-behaved scientific questions whose answers merit the high dignity of proof. This transforming is the work of philosophy. Thus on this definition the proper subject matter of philosophy will be questionable questions, questions so important that we find ourselves compelled to ask them, but so vague and troublesome that we cannot say what would count as

1

answering them. The philosopher's task will be to theorize about these questionable questions, analyzing them, refining and redefining them, transforming them into sensible, tasteful, fruitful questions, questions answerable perhaps by experts of one sort or another, perhaps by laymen, or perhaps demonstrably unanswerable.

Given these terms and this definition of philosophy, we can now say what this essay is about. If philosophy is the science of questions, then one way to give an exposition and defense of a set of philosophical principles will be to set those principles to work upon an especially questionable question, using them to transform it from something with which we feel intellectually uncomfortable into something with which we feel intellectually at home and at ease. Clearly, the more questionable the question, the more plausibility must accrue to the principles: if they can make sense of *that*, we shall want to say, then there must be something to them. In this essay, we shall construct a philosophical theory of the question, "What is love?" While other questions may or may not be more questionable—a vague issue, surely—unquestionably this is a most questionable question: diffuse, messy, embarrassing, the sort of question one might ask a priest, prostitute, or psychoanalyst, expecting to receive more comfort than enlightenment from the answer. The reader—whose mind I shall from time to time presume to read—unquestionably thinks this question in the end really unanswerable or (what comes to the same) answerable however many ways one may wish. Here, then, we have what seems a proper subject matter for the science of questions, a question at once messy, vital, and apparently unanswerable, indeed, a question that we somehow feel *should* not have a real (that is, a demonstrable) answer—but one that we nevertheless persist in asking. Surely a philosophy that can make sense of such a question will have demonstrated that its principles are sound, fresh, and lively.

Our objective, then, is to defend a philosophy by showing it in action, putting its principles to work upon the questionable question "What is love?" Besides being especially questionable, this question has the additional advantage of being relatively concrete. Such philosophical familiars as "How are mind and body related to one another?", "What is being?", "Does the Right differ from the Good?", and the like, are well institutionalized. These questions have become abstract, for we have learned how to pose them abstractly, that is, how to pose them within the confines of philosophy, in abstraction from the concreteness of everyday life. When we are asked how mind and body are related to one another, we know the question invites us to participate in a theoretical inquiry, and we are prepared to grant the questioner's theoretical intentions. "What is love?" is not so neat. We are unsure what sort of inquiry the question proposes, and we wonder whether we are invited to be edifying or gushy, raunchy or sentimental, clinical or cynical. Our intentions in this essay, however, are straightforwardly theoretical—a claim which only the argument of the essay itself can justify. We want to construct a theory of the question "What is love?" Because this theory intends merely to be a theory of the question, we are not required to answer the question, but only to make good theoretical sense of it. One excellent test of a theory of a question, however, is the ability of the theory to answer that question, in whatever sense the question deserves an answer. With that qualification, we shall in fact prove what love is.

Starting Point and Method of the Theory

The theory of a subject is the set of proofs that will properly decide questions about that subject matter. Our subject matter is the question "What is love?" We want our philosophical theory to show us how to transform that initially vague and troublesome question into something much clearer and more manageable. Exactly what such a theory is can be shown only by the argument itself in which the theory is constructed. So far we have declared only that our intentions are entirely theoretical, that is, that we wish to solve a certain intellectual puzzle, not to elevate sentiments, reform morals, nor counsel the distressed—worthy objectives, but not ours. And we have a secondary objective, namely, to prove what love is.

Granted these objectives and these theoretical intentions, we need to determine where our argument should start and to what sort of evidence it should appeal, especially in its beginning. And since a clear objective can be clearly stated, we should also state when the argument will be entitled to conclude.

The English noun "love" identifies our subject matter. Unlike "mass point," "catalepsy," "reagent," or "tessitura," "love" is not a technical term but a layman's word, part of ordinary language and everyday life. The layman's theoretically innocent understanding of "What is love?" must be our starting point. That understanding is the understanding of a certain word, a dismayingly diffuse noun. Here we make an assumption that will govern the remainder of the argument. We shall assume that by "love" the layman means primarily *romantic* love; that is, we shall assume that the many meanings of the word center around that one, so that were that central meaning made clear, then the word's many other meanings could be clarified with comparative ease. In an entirely preliminary way, we may identify romantic love as love where a sexual involvement is possible— differentiating it thus from love of mother, God, country, Yale, cats and dogs, and so on. Of course this large assumption is a hypothesis that the argument must justify eventually, and this preliminary identification must be replaced by something much better.

We shall also assume that it is a fact of experience that the layman thinks

"What is [romantic] love?" an unanswerable question. As we shall see, our theory must be answerable for this fact. We may note first that the word itself cannot be the cause of the question's supposed unanswerability. Whether or not laymen and laywomen[1] think they can say what they mean by "love," they do use the word to communicate with one another, managing their affairs by means of it, relying upon it to articulate to themselves what the world is like and what each of them is like also. Offhand, there seems no reason to suppose "love" causes more confusion than comparably multipurpose words such as "good" and "meaning." "Love" may not be sharply defined after the fashion of a technical term, but if we make allowances for the wide variety of its uses, it seems definite enough in meaning to be a successful instrument of communication, and that, after all, is what words are for.

But the layman does not understand "What is love?" to ask merely "What is the meaning of the English noun 'love'?" Dictionaries answer that question. U. S. Grant wrote that he was taught as a schoolboy that a noun is the name of a thing, and he believed it. The layman's understanding of the question is ontological: he thinks the noun "love" is the name of some real thing, and the question asks what that real thing is. In philosophy, this understanding of the "What is ——?" question form has a long history, reaching back to Plato's early Socratic dialogues. When Socrates asks "What is courage?" or "What is friendship?" he invokes the distinction between what a thing really is and what it only seems to be. Generals such as Laches and Nicias (in the *Laches*) can tell courage when they encounter instances of it, but cannot give a theory of it, a systematic, defensible account of what holds together these many instances and makes each of them an instance of courage rather than of something else. In other words, they cannot say what courage is "really."

"What is love *really*?" suggests, however, that the answer should be expressed in some technical vocabulary. "Really, love is the displacement of energy from the frustrated desire to obtain exclusive possession of the ideal mother."[2] Freudian technical terms such as "frustration," "displacement," and "mother fixation," on the other hand, are defined by special experiences, experiences available only to psychoanalytic clinicians, and it seems rather arbitrary to begin a theory of the layman's innocent understanding of "What is love?" simply by assuming that those special experiences are a reliable guide to it. Perhaps we may find eventually that we should deed our question, or some revised version of it, over to some special science; at this stage in the argument, we do not know which special science we should choose. Like the terms Socrates defines (including "love" itself in the *Symposium*), "love" possesses its meaning in the first instance not in the clinic, the lecture room, or the laboratory, but out in the street, that is, in everyday social intercourse. Our theory's starting point, then, should be the commonplace use of the word and the commonplace experience of the thing. These should be our primary data. Art historians, who have actually examined the original paintings, are entitled to develop theories we laymen must accept in part on faith, for we have not had those special experiences. Advanced mathematics, by contrast, is about the adding, subtracting, multiplying, and dividing of high-school algebra, operations familiar to everyone who has been to high school. Our primary data are also forms of experience and patterns of discourse familiar to everyone. We begin by taking "love" to be the name of a mysterious, intimate, incommunicable, but unmistakable feeling and by interpreting "What is love?" to ask "What is that feeling?" because this is how the layman takes the word and the question.

Interpreting the question in this way implies that the answer is irretrievably hidden within the individual. Love, like the taste of turtle soup, must be experienced to be understood. Those who have had the experience know what the word means, those who have not are necessarily ignorant of it; and even those who have experienced love have no sure and certain way to determine whether their individual experiences are the same or different. If the question is interpreted in this way, then it is in principle unanswerable, and, in that sense at least, a bad and fruitless question.

The balance of our argument will be about this initial interpretation of "What is love?" This starting point also determines the method of the argument. We begin with a supposedly unanswerable question. The answer may be altogether indefinite or hidden away within the individual, but the question itself is a definite question. Its unanswerability is a property it shares with other questions that in their own ways also are unanswerable. In other words, the question may lead nowhere, but it leads from somewhere: a background of tacit assumptions about language, thought, and the world generates our question's supposed unanswerability. The strategy of our argument, then, should be to consider figure and ground together, trying to see how this unanswerability results from their relationship. In Part I, we shall examine love as we think of it in everyday life. We think of it as a feeling. "What is love?" asks "What is that feeling?" Love as a feeling, however, appears against a background of promises, commitments, and policies, these in turn against a background of agreements, understandings, and contracts. Romantical agreements stand out against that ultimate concatenation of human agreements we call "society," and so in Part II we shall examine love as a social institution and the question "Which institution is it?" This examination is an exercise in sociology, and so Part III will ask what is the society that is the first principle of sociological inquiry. The "society" of social science stands in contrast to the "nature" of natural science. These first principles of inquiry, however, figure against a ground which is the activity of inquiry itself. If they seem vast and obscure, it by contrast is something we do, and do together, and can therefore understand. This collective activity, theoretical inquiry, in turn stands out against collective activity as such or in general. This again is "society," and so we shall conclude by saying what society is and what part love plays in it.

Starting from romantic love in everyday life, then, we shall regress again and again upon our own assumptions, casting an ever wider and deeper net, each combination of figure and ground emerging on a new ground of its own. The "how" of this emergence will differ from each transformation of the question to the next. From this series of transformations of "What is love?" one may draw a conclusion about philosophy itself. It comes, as a conclusion should, at the end.

While one should not ask that a philosopher's method prescribe the detailed course of his argument, one may legitimately demand that he state in advance when the argument will be entitled to conclude. Criteria for the conclusion of this argument are implicit, clearly, in the two assumptions that constitute its starting point. When we ask "What is love?" we intend "What is ——?" in its traditional philosophical sense, the sense in which Socrates asks "What is courage?" in the *Laches* and "What is justice?" in the *Republic*. Our inquiry is ontological. We want to know whether and how love exists, or what kind of being love has. Thus whatever else it may accomplish, our theory at once of love and of "What is love?" must be an ontological theory; it must evaluate the reality of love in comparison to the other things we think are real. Such a demand seems entirely unfulfillable, and that appearance determines our second criterion: our theory must explain why we, as laymen, initially thought such a theory quite impossible. After constructing our theory, we may then reflect on what we have done, drawing a conclusion about philosophy.

Part I
The Concept of Love

§1 Words, Thoughts, and Things: The Lay Semantics of Love

The layman thinks "What is love?" asks what a certain emotion, sentiment, or feeling is. Love is a feeling, and so the question asks "What is that feeling?" The layman thinks the question is in the end unanswerable because he thinks the feeling in the end is inexpressible.

We begin with this layman's reaction to the question. While we shall react, and in a sense react adversely, to this reaction, "layman" is not pejorative and no disrespect is implied. Whatever else we may be, all of us are laymen. Our self-awareness as laymen is both the evidence and the agency to which we appeal as philosophical theorists: the respect we owe this self-awareness is the respect we owe ourselves. If, then, we find the theoretical basis of the layman's reaction naive and unsatisfactory, it must not be supposed that we think the layman—ourselves!—stupid or perverse or negligent, but rather that we suspect something deeper is afoot. Indeed, this self-respect prescribes that we should proceed in this Part I in a leisurely, digressive fashion, obtaining a feeling for our evidence, allowing our theoretical principles to emerge in a natural way from our everyday experience. Moreover, love is, as the Freudians say, "highly cathected," a serious business. This seriousness threatens our objectivity, and we must develop tools for dealing with it. Fortunately, romantic love has its lighter side, especially in the drama of courtship. This suggests that we should begin with that lighter side, preserving a certain lightness of tone, gradually working our way into the serious heart of the question as our theoretical principles develop. Patience is asked of the philosophical reader.

We take our first step into theory in this section, articulating the implicit semantical theory which seems to underly the layman's skeptical reaction to the prospect of theorizing about love. We shall see in §2 that even for the layman, that reaction is excessive, and so in §3 we shall examine love as a feeling directly. What we say about love as philosophical theorists may be practically inconsequential, but the words of love we speak to one another in everyday life have real consequences. So we have ways of testing the reality of one another's feelings, and those tests—we shall call them "policies"—are tested in turn by contracts. A "test" implies a theory, and so the layman has a theory after all: love is really a kind of contractual exchange. The layman is inclined to say, however, that that is not what he means by "love"—the rhetoric is entirely wrong. The distinctions on which that inclination is based are examined in §4.

"No one can say what love is." But why not? "Because love is a feeling, the most intimate and profound of the emotions, something one must have experienced for oneself if one is to understand it." But supposing one has experienced it, cannot one then communicate what one has experienced? "No, not really. It's far too personal to be expressed. Heightened discourse—poetry, music, fiction—may suggest what it's like, but suggestion is not expression, and ultimately love remains something each individual knows only within himself, if he knows it at all."

This conventional point of view depends upon an implied contrast and an implicit semantical theory. The contrast is between what is public, objective, demonstrable, and communicable, on the one hand, and what is private, subjective, indemonstrable, and incommunicable, on the other hand. The theory concerns how words, thoughts, and things are related to one another. Words, the layman supposes, are arbitrary signs for thoughts, and thoughts are mental pictures of things. We English-speakers say "love," Frenchmen say *l'amour*, Germans *die Liebe*. All three words refer to the same thing, express the same idea. But they are arbitrary signs for the idea they express. Had English developed differently, "hate" might have meant what "love" now means, just as we might have learned to count "one, three, two" instead of "one, two, three," reversing our names for the second and third positive integers.

An idea is expressed by "love," the same idea expressed to a Frenchman by *l'amour* and to a German by *die Liebe*. To say this is merely to assert that the word has a meaning. But what is this meaning? That is, what does the word mean?

One's natural impulse is to answer, "A feeling, namely, the feeling you have when . . . ," describing in the ellipsis some experience intended to epitomize the feeling. Here we differ, however. One person's tea party is another's orgy: what epitomizes love to you may mean something quite different to me. By definition, different individuals have different experiences, therefore different memories, therefore different associations of words

8

with thoughts, different ideas of what words mean. Because our experiences are often similar, we can usually communicate with one another. In the case of public, objective, demonstrable things such as numbers, weights and measures, and rules of grammar, this similarity approaches identity and communication tends to be relatively efficient. Feelings such as love, on the other hand, differ so widely from individual to individual that communication about them is always to some extent superficial. No matter how assiduously we may try, the mere and necessary fact that we are different individuals who have had different experiences forbids our ever fully communicating. Necessarily, feelings are "private."

In this conventional, implicit theory, one's concept of love is the image of certain feelings and experiences. Your experiences of love and the feelings you have must differ from my feelings and experiences. Therefore we will have different concepts of love. Had we all the same concept, then presumably our communication could be complete, the point being that in this implicit theory, what thwarts communication is not the absence of a common feeling, but the absence of a common concept.

Now an implicit theory, a theory-in-effect, is a straw man. It would be idle to press it for details, since it is already a theorist's interpretation of lay thought, speech, and behavior. Here the layman does not have a theory, but has instead a very firm conviction that love is a feeling that cannot fruitfully be theorized about. The layman himself will meet challenges to that conviction not with theory, but with impatience. Therefore, although there are a number of well-worn philosophical objections to the lay semantical theory sketched out here, it would serve no purpose to pursue them. The implicit semantical theory does not give the real reason why the layman thinks theorizing about love impossible—we shall see later that the real reason is entirely different—but gives instead a theoretical work-up of an inarticulate reaction. In order to deal with that reaction at all, we must treat it as if it concealed a theory; otherwise, we should be talking back to silence. Our theory-sketch tries to give not the layman's real reasons, but what would seem to him his reasons were he to take the first step into theory. It is in that sense an interpretation—as we hope, a fair interpretation.

§2 The Incommunicability of Love: A First Look

In so far as the layman may be said implicitly to theorize about such private feelings as love, what he theorizes is that proof and theory about those feelings is impossible. By definition, a theory is a public thing. If the layman is correct, "What is love?" is a futile question, for in order to answer it, theory would have to reach into those private areas from which it is necessarily excluded. Those areas are not beyond the reach of theory simply because certain feelings are private, however, but rather because the privacy of a feeling implies the privacy also of the idea or concept of it. Where we all have the same concept—mathematics is the cliché example—there we can fruitfully theorize. Where our ideas must differ, however, theory must be impotent. The problem seems to be not that the feeling of love cannot be conceptualized, but that there are at least as many concepts of the feeling as there are individuals who have felt it.

What is impossible—in this conventional view—is not to have the concept of love but rather to communicate it. Evidently even behind the veil of privacy there is a difference between those who have the concept—we should perhaps say "such a concept"—and those who do not. The former have had the appropriate experiences; the latter have not, and their astonishment upon discovering that the world contains such a feeling as love is often celebrated in fiction.

What it might mean to have the incommunicable concept of an incommunicable feeling seems obscure at best. Since this particular case seems so obscure, it might be well to turn aside for a moment in order to examine what in general we mean by "having a concept" and how someone who has a particular concept differs from someone who does not. Here we move onto territory familiar to philosophers.

The concept of "love" stands between the word "love" and the feeling. One way to identify the concept is as what the word means, for then we can say that someone who knows what the word means has the concept. Another way is as what someone who has felt the feeling should be expected to have and someone who has not had it should be expected to lack. If the layman had to say what the concept in this latter sense is, he would probably say it is a mental image. It would be unfair to take this identification too seriously, for what a concept is is a problem not for laymen but for philosophers, who are supposed to theorize about such matters. Moreover, there is in ordinary usage the important clue that, at least sometimes and for some purposes, what we need to know about a concept is not what it is, but what it does, what its function is, how those who have it are better off than those who do not. Consider:

Instructor (to *Student Mechanic*): "No, no, *advance* the fast idle; don't turn it back! The mixture is supposed to get richer, not leaner. If you don't have the concept of how a carburetor works, how can you expect to tune a carburetor?"

Someone who has the concept of a carburetor knows how a carburetor is supposed to work. There are, of course, degrees of having the concept. One might know only that the carburetor is where air and gasoline are mixed, but be unable to go under the hood and find it. Or one might know how to find the carburetor and also how to tell when the carburetor is malfunctioning, but still need a mechanic to repair it—the plight of the average motorist. Or one might be a mechanic and capable of repairing some kinds of carburetor, or even almost any kind, but be incapable of designing a carburetor. Or one might be an automotive engineer who can design carburetors. Perhaps this series ends here.

In this usage, having the idea or concept of a carburetor—to whatever degree—gives one a power or ability one would otherwise lack, and the higher the degree, the greater the power. We may note also that even though "carburetor" is a noun and a carburetor a readily picturable object, having the concept of a carburetor need not involve entertaining any particular mental images. If we ask the automotive engineer or the master mechanic what a carburetor looks like, he may reply, "There are hundreds of different designs." Although he does not associate any particular imagery with "carburetor," it need not follow that he cannot repair any carburetor put before him. Indeed, the mechanic for whom "carburetor" suggests particular imagery may be handicapped, for he may be able to repair only carburetors of a single design.

The carburetor example suggests the analogy made famous by Wittgenstein: a concept is like a tool for doing a certain job. Saying what the concept is means showing what job it does, what power or ability it confers, or what it is used for.[1]

Applying this analogy to the concept of love, we recognize that persons do use it to organize complicated social relationships. Someone lacking the concept would find those relationships unintelligible. Were he himself suddenly caught up in the social whirl, we should expect him to be as seriously disadvantaged as the bewildered farmer who stumbles into the midst of army maneuvers.

The tool analogy assumes that a concept is a means to an end. The motorist wants the trouble-free use of his car. The concept of a carburetor is as handy for attaining this end as is a socket set or a tire iron. Loving, however, is supposed to be an end in itself, not a means to some other end. That distinction appears to be no small part of what we mean when we call love a feeling. "Marsha," we ask, "What are you trying to accomplish, being in love with John? What's your purpose?" Marsha, quite properly offended, replies, "I don't love him for a purpose, I just love him, that's all." The idea that love is a feeling blocks the "Why?" question (in the sense in which "Why?" means "For what purpose?"). It also casts doubt on the applicability of the tool analogy to the concept of love. "Why do you have the concept of a carburetor?" is a sensible question, although a very peculiar one, for it has the straightforward answer, "Because I have a carburetor, and I need to know how and what to do when it doesn't work right." By contrast, "Why do you have the concept of love?" is not at all a clear question. Consider the following exchange:

Sidney: "Why do you have the concept of love?"

John: "An odd question! I suppose because I am in love—with Marsha—and I like to think about what I feel."

Sidney: "So the purpose of the concept is to enable you to cope with the feeling. But what is the purpose of the feeling?"

John: "That is an ambiguous question. On a purely personal level, I haven't any ulterior motive for loving Marsha, but the feeling is its own end. My analyst, on the other hand, might tell you I love her because she reminds me of my mother, or something of the sort. Or if you're asking, as you well might be, why people in general fall in love, then I suppose the answer is evolutionary: love is nature's means for perpetuating the species, right?"

John knows that he himself may not honorably love Marsha for a purpose. The feeling that he himself should not experience as purposive, however, may be seen by his analyst to be subconsciously purposive, and this subconscious purposiveness is unobjectionable. And nature—evolution—may have a general purpose where it would be wrong for John to have a particular one. The concept of a feeling, on the other hand, will have a purpose that is determined for it by the feeling, for a feeling always calls for a purposive reaction. Conceptualizing one's feelings in this sense is a requirement for survival: given the feeling of hunger, one must know that, what, and how one should eat. Or consider:

New Instructor (who drops the chalk, can't close his briefcase, and acts flustered and distraught): "I teach my first class in five minutes, and I feel just awful."

Senior Professor: "Don't let it bother you—just a touch of stage fright, that's all. You'll be fine. Only remember to talk slowly."

The new instructor does not know what to call the feeling he has, and the senior professor tells him at once what to call it and what to do about it, or, as we may say, what policy to adopt for coping with it. Any feeling seems less strange and more manageable once a label has been attached to it. Thus consider the following dialogue from science fiction:

X15 (from Mars): "I don't know what to do; I have this strange new feeling whenever Marsha is around."

Earthman: "Why, X15, I do believe you're in love."

X15: "Oh, Earthman, what should I do?"

X15 wants to know what policy to adopt in order to bring his strange new feeling to a favorable outcome. Typically, Earthman will say, "So *tell* Marsha you love her," or "First, use your death ray on John," or "Why don't you take her some of those pretty Martian flowers?"

The Man from Mars is entirely imaginary, and yet anyone—at least anyone who has ever watched "Star Trek"—knows how to play through this scene, this little dramatic bit. Evidently, concepts such as the concept of love are communicated, broadcast among the public by being dramatized in this way. We urban, Western, late twentieth-century folk have our peculiar sense of what is dramatically convincing. An older time might have played through the X15 a bit differently:

X15: "I don't know what to do; I have this strange new feeling whenever Marsha is around."

Earthman: "Thou art in great peril, X15. The Tempter seeks thy soul. He would fill thee with lust for Marsha the better to ensnare thee. Come, let us fall upon our knees and pray together."

The feeling of love should not be a means to an end; but the concept, in the sense discussed, obviously is a means, and the end to which it is a means is determined by the feeling. Here we may note that our reservations about the communicability of the concept fall immediately away, as the many varieties of advice to the lovelorn testify. The feeling may be incommunicable, but what to do about the feeling is eminently communicable and often communicated. Clearly, the concept of love—in this sense of "concept"—is culturally relative, a concept that our culture perpetuates from generation to generation, just as we perpetuate our concepts of a good time or a successful career, concepts that are fundamental to our sense of what is dramatically tasteful and convincing.

In so far as "What is love?" asks "What is the feeling of love?" the question is unanswerable—or so the layman thinks, at least. But in so far as the concept of love is what confers the ability to cope with the feeling, then even though the feeling may be incommunicable, the concept certainly is not, and in that sense, "What is love?" has an answer. Even from a lay point of view, then, prospects for a theory of love are not altogether hopeless. A "theory" in this sense would not be about the feeling, but about how to cope with it. How to cope with it is a problem that may be faced on various levels of sophistication and with the aid of technical information from biology, psychology, sociology, history, and other disciplines besides. But it is a reasonably well-defined problem with definite, demonstrable solutions. What we think is "the thing to say" about love is characteristic of our culture and has a history which can be traced back to Eleanor of Aquitaine and the medieval Courts of Love.[2] Here tradition provides a solid basis for genuine theorizing.

Apparently we are not altogether in earnest about love's incommunicability. In at least one sense, the concept of love is quite communicable and provides the basis for a series of theories ranging from popular advice to the lovelorn to the history, psychology, and sociology of this advice. Even in their sophisticated historical, psychological, and sociological dimensions, however, these theories seem to depend upon the putative properties of an incommunicable, intensely personal feeling, which seems a questionable ground for proof. They take the ontology of love for granted. Does such a feeling really exist? Perhaps we are not altogether in earnest about it, either.

§3 Love as a Feeling

The commonplace assumption that love is a feeling is our starting point and the first item of evidence on which our theory is based. We proceed in a leisurely, informal fashion, trying to obtain a sense for our evidence before theorizing about it, for we do not know yet what sort of theory would be appropriate. Were we to begin by locating love within an elaborate theory of the emotions, we should not be allowing the facts to speak for themselves. We shall take our first step into theory in this section.

Sometimes we oppose feeling to thought: "Try not to think about what you're doing [when you back the truck into the alley or make the incision in the heart itself]; just feel your way along." Where love is concerned, however, the opposite of feeling would appear to be not thought, but action. If Marsha declares, "I have decided to fall in love with John," we will think her a hard-hearted creature with designs on John's money or social position. One can no more deliberately fall in love than one can deliberately stumble, a stumble being one kind of accidental fall. We speak of feelings, sentiments, and emotions as passivities, things that happen to us rather than things that we do. We are *struck* or *seized* by panic or remorse, *overcome* by fear, *driven* by lust—these metaphors picture us forced to feel. Besides passivity, "feeling" typically suggests brevity: we are forced from our normal course, but suddenly and temporarily.

Often emotions call for actions as responses to them. Fear prompts me to seek safety, resentment to take revenge, joy to prolong what I feel. And many feelings have objects: fear is usually fear *of* some danger, remorse remorse *over* some loss, and so on. Romantic love is love of some particular person. When Marsha says, "I'm in love!" she invites the question, "With whom?" Feelings whose objects are particular persons we may call "social feelings."

Social feelings tend to give rise to policies, long-term plans designed to cope with the feeling. When Rosie cruelly offends her, a wave of hatred engulfs Marsha. (Hydraulic metaphors for feelings are common.) She may take this sudden feeling seriously, or she may merely wait for it to pass, depending, of course, on many circumstances. Suppose she takes it seriously and develops a long-lasting hatred of Rosie. Then when asked how she feels about Rosie, she may say, "Oh, I just hate her!" Hatred in this sense, however, is not a short-run feeling, but a long-run plan of action: Marsha intends to denounce Rosie to whoever will listen, to thwart Rosie's ambitions, to steal her friends, and so on. What in its beginnings fits the model of a feeling, a sudden, short-run passivity, an involuntary being-overcome, develops in the long run into a policy, a voluntarily adopted, designed plan of action in which Marsha persists in spite of the momentary ebbs and flows (another hydraulic metaphor) of feeling. "For an instant there, where the party was really wild and she was giving her demonstration of belly dancing, I almost forgot how much I hate Rosie." Here Marsha's commitment to a policy prompts her to ignore what she temporarily feels.

And so the obvious point of this discussion: feelings and the policies to which they give rise are often called by the same name, hence we tend to confuse them with one another.

When this observation is applied to love, John sees Marsha's mouse-brown hair and sexy figure. A feeling overcomes him: he loves her. In time he tells her, "Marsha, I love you!" Marsha does not take him to have given her a psychological report about a temporary feeling-state. Should she discover him, moments later, embracing Rosie, she will conclude he lied when he said he loved her, and he will not be able to justify himself by saying feelings come and go (although feelings do just that). What she takes him to have promised is not a sudden flush of feeling, but an enduring commitment to action, a policy. To be sure, this policy originates in a feeling and depends upon that feeling, but it is supposed to be a far more lasting and reliable affair. John has less than full control over his feelings, or so the rhetoric of feeling implies; but he can control his policies, and therefore Marsha hopes she can count on him.

As a social feeling, love aims for a response from its object. John's declaration of love is not a psychological report on a par with "I have a headache" or "Don't do that, it really frightens me." He tells Marsha he loves her because he wants her to love him. Love wants to be requited, returned, reciprocated. Here too we deal not with feelings but with policies, although these policies are supposed to have their basis in feeling. When Marsha says, "I love you too, John," she promises to adopt a policy that intermeshes with the policy John promises, and we may say that a compact or contract or agreement is formed, a set of mutual obligations and expectations. Of course such an agreement is at most morally binding and the parties will in all likelihood be unable to state its terms in detail. But they can tell when it has been violated, as for example when Marsha sees John embracing Rosie.

In this first step toward defining love, we have moved from what are said to be private, incommunicable feelings to contracts, agreements, or understandings, items which in their very nature are public and communicable.

When Marsha says, "Dear John, I'm so sorry, I don't love you, I love Sidney instead," both John and Marsha understand well enough what was asked of her, what she declined, and to what she would agree with Sidney, should he ask it. There are variations from circle to circle and couple to couple—some copulate, some hold hands—but the difference between "I love you" and "I hate you" or "Buzz off, you creep" is surely as clear as it needs to be. And of course we were not born with a knowledge of how to make nor what to expect from declarations of love, just as we were not born speaking English and behaving like Americans. Our culture is the common school in which we all learned the same language and the same social ceremonies. We are, as we say, "socialized."

A substantial part of the socialization of an American consists in learning rules for forming and managing contractual bonds of romantic love. Since even otherwise innocent children learn that there is such a feeling, that it should play a major part in their lives, and how in detail they should relate to one another in terms of it, love can scarcely be mysterious and incommunicable. Something that is the commonest theme of vicarious experience, of movies, television, popular music, and light and heavy fiction and drama would appear to be, if anything, excessively obvious.

When John says, at a time and in a manner weighted with feeling, "I love you, Marsha," this is hardly an original move on his part. Marsha knows what he means and what she is entitled to expect should she accept his offer. He promises a long-run course of action, a policy. Such a policy is supposed to be based on what he feels, but the connection is complex and indirect, for policies as often dictate feelings as reflect them. Whatever "I love you, Marsha" may mean to John and Marsha—and in free-thinking or disreputable circles, it may promise little, or much, but not for very long—policy contrasts with feeling as the lasting contrasts with the momentary. John promises affectionate feelings, but also, and more to the point, he promises to repress momentary spasms of revulsion, disgust, annoyance, and the like. And he promises also to repress any feeling for Rosie that might threaten temporarily to overcome his feeling for Marsha.

When we say feelings are "private," we mean at least that they can be concealed, at most that they must forever remain to some extent concealed. We are examining the latter extreme. We should observe that concealment is defined by contrast to revelation and that what in everyday life we take to reveal and test feelings is faithfulness to policies. Again, the point is that the time scale of the two differs. For an hour, a week, a month, a year John can conceal his inner contempt for Marsha's character and his lust for her body (or her wealth, her social position, or whatever). On the other hand, if after sixty years of marriage and unfailingly devoted, affectionate behavior, John whispers on his deathbed, "I never loved her," we are likelier to think him delirious or distracted or senile than sincere and correct. We say that actions speak louder than words, and this seems a reasonable thing to say, for acting out a policy takes much longer than merely promising one.

Is there, then, such a feeling as love? Surely what cannot be felt sincerely cannot be felt insincerely either, and therefore cannot be felt at all. The sincerity of feelings of love is tested by the policies that lovers promise. Therefore if there were no loving policies then there could be no loving feelings. Further, a policy that cannot be faithfully maintained cannot be unfaithfully maintained either, and therefore cannot be maintained at all. Contracts, mutual promises, determine what will count as faithfulness in love. Lovers' promises are moral actions governed by rules we all know and in general accept. There are differences in detail, but in detail only. Inner feelings and inner intentions are both tested, and therefore also defined, by contracts that are acts of communication, and as such by nature public, open, and unmysterious. Love can be a private, mysterious, incommunicable feeling only by also being far more than merely that.

"Is love a feeling?" appears to be a psychological question. The evidence upon which we have drawn, however, is not psychological, but linguistic and moral. We have drawn not upon the scientific study of human behavior, but instead upon how we talk about our thoughts, feelings, and actions, especially when we pass moral judgment on them. Here we have no need of scientific information, whether from psychology or elsewhere. Correct grammar is determined by how *we* talk, and any native speaker of English is as much an authority as any other, for in grammatical disputes, ultimately we appeal to the native speaker's sense of his own language. Similarly, correct behavior is determined by how *we* judge, and any sane, adult American is as much an authority as any other, for in moral disputes, we ultimately appeal to the sane adult's sense of right and wrong. One may reassure oneself that this is not hyperbole by reflecting on how we think persons can be "talented." In grading livestock or tuning stringed instruments, we ordinary folk must defer to the talented. There can be no such persons as the "morally talented," however, for if there were, then the rest of us could excuse our misdeeds by saying we lack their talent.

Since in this section we take the first step toward a theory of love, we should look with some care at what we have done. We still do not know what love is, but we have a better idea of how to interpret "What is love?" sensibly. If policies test feelings and contracts test policies, then clearly we should concentrate on what lovers promise one another rather than on what they feel. We see that we do not need to impose some theory of our own devising upon everyday behavior. A theory of love, or a theory-in-effect, is already there: those who stand to gain or lose from others' professions of love already possess well-defined means for determining the truth or falsity of those professions. Love is said to be mysterious, but the contractual consequences of claiming to have been smitten by it are the opposite of mysterious. A contract is by nature open and accessible, for its nature is to be communicated, to be proposed by one person to another in terms familiar to both, then either accepted or rejected so that both know which happened, and if accepted, then either kept or broken by standards also familiar to both. The function of a contract is to stand between individuals, not to be hidden inside them. Here we deal not with the dark secrets of the psyche, but with the fundamental moral information we require of one another. Thus if—as a rough first approximation, merely—we define a "society" as the largest set of individuals any one of whom can understand the behavior of any other without the assistance of an anthropologist, then the fact that each of us possesses this moral sense is what makes us a single society.

Finally, although it may be unilluminating to call love a feeling, and although, as we have argued, love in fact is a feeling only by also being much more than merely a feeling, these conclusions as they stand seem shallow. We noted in §2 that our purpose in calling love a feeling seems to be less to achieve psychological accuracy than to block questions and guide behavior. To say only that love is not merely a feeling neglects the possibility that we can learn as much from the fact that we are trained to call love a feeling as we do from the fact that love does not neatly fit this classification.

§4 Love as Contractual

For our purposes, a "social relationship" is a morally regulated two-person relationship where each party knows he has that particular relationship to the other and knows that the other knows this too. There will be an *exchange*, that is, each will expect certain behaviors from the other and will think himself obliged to behave appropriately in return. A husband, for example, will entertain complex expectations of his wife's behavior and will regard himself as obligated to her in many ways, but only on condition that she take up an appropriately wifely set of expectations and obligations toward him. Strangers passing on the street owe one another little—civil inattention, free passage, "free goods" such as the time or a light, warning of extraordinary perils such as a collapsed bridge or a shoot-out—and expect as little from one another.[3] Should either party to a social relationship seriously fail to meet his obligations to the other or seriously appear to entertain expectations that the other does not feel obliged to fulfil, then the relationship will become unstable and insupportable, for neither party will know how to interpret it.

What I have said using the economic term "exchange" could have been said using the dramaturgical metaphor implied by "role." Or I could have spoken simply of "agreement," the point being that a social relationship is stable when the parties agree about those matters that are essential to it, and especially about the identity it assigns to each of them.

Suppose John and Marsha are friends, but each secretly loves the other and secretly hopes the feeling is returned. Suppose then that with a full heart, John says, "Marsha, I love you!" and Marsha replies, "Oh, John, I love you too!" We will agree that this mutual profession changes their relationship. They were "just friends," entitled perhaps to preferential rights to one another's company, a good report to third parties, and various minor services, and if asked, either would acknowledge having agreed to that. Their new agreement substantially enlarges their obligations to and expectations from one another. It is just the sort of thing we tend to notice ("Oh, Rosie, guess what! John and Marsha are in love!"), whereas the fact that their previous relationship also involved an agreement is the sort of thing we tend not to notice. We may speak, then, of a "contract," "compact," "understanding," or "agreement," recognizing that these same terms could have been applied to their previous relationship as friends.

A "contract" in the most literal sense is a legally binding agreement, often expressed in a signed and notarized document, for the exchange of goods or services. However, if legal contracts are hard, cold, and dry, lover's compacts are usually thought to have the contrary qualities. Even though the contract concept applies quite generally to any social relationship, we are inclined to find its application to love a trifle distasteful. To conceive of loving relationships as contractual exchanges seems insensitive, somehow, to what we really intend in those relationships. These misgivings are worth exploring in detail, for they depend on three distinctions that are useful for determining the disciplinary assignment of a theory of love.

§4.1 Primary and Secondary Relationships   The distinction between primary and secondary relationships, in various forms and under various names, has a long history. The version given here is sociological and is ultimately derived from Charles Horton Cooley.[4] As we have seen, every social relationship involves an exchange. We shall call a social relationship "primary" if the goods exchanged are supposed to be unique and essential to the exchangers, "secondary" if they are supposed to be duplicatable and inessential to the exchangers. A friendship is a primary relationship, since one's friends are supposed to like one for oneself. The buyer and seller of a car have a secondary relationship, since the attractiveness of the car to the buyer has nothing directly to do with its having been the property of the seller, while the seller will take anyone's money. A secondary relationship involves the exchange of duplicatable goods, goods to which a monetary

value can be assigned, and one is morally entitled to refuse an offered bargain on the chance that a better offer may turn up. Following Kant, we may say that primary relationships involve the exchange of things that possess *dignity*, secondary relationships the exchange of things that possess *price*.[5]

Persons who bear a primary relationship to one another are sometimes said to form a "primary group" (Cooley's original term), for example, a clique, a children's gang, or a family. Secondary groups are sometimes called "instrumental groups," for the value of the group (or of the relationships, to say the same) to its members will reside not in the group itself, but in other values the group is instrumental for achieving. Thus a business concern is an instrumental group, for its employees work (officially, at least) not in order to enjoy one another's company nor to bask in one another's approval, but to make money.

Even these few examples will suggest that this is a complex distinction. We began by supposing that social relationships can be divided into two groups: on the one hand, those based on honor and dishonor, affection and disaffection; on the other, those based on profit and loss. As soon as we actually name some of these relationships, however, this division ceases to seem neatly dichotomous. Even the archetypically impersonal secondary relationship between the buyer of a ticket and the seller behind the box-office window has its primary aspect, for each is positively obliged not to take personal notice of the other. Thus should the seller comment on the buyer's necktie or Gay Lib button, the buyer would have the right to be offended. Primary relationships, on the other hand, may be instrumental, even essential to life, as is the mother's relationship to her small child—who nevertheless is supposed to love her for herself, not merely for the things she does for him. (We think he would do wrong to leave her for someone who promises to do more.) Interpreting the division this way, we may speak of the primary and secondary "sides" or "aspects" of a relationship, and we can argue that every relationship will have both, though one or the other will be more noticeable.

A social relationship is a set of mutually relevant and collectively enforced obligations and expectations. Strictly, we should speak of "an instance of a social relationship," for the relationship itself will be a universal, and the parties to it will draw upon a moral fact well defined in advance. When Marsha becomes a mother, she knows how mothers are supposed to behave, and she will train little Marvin to behave toward her as a child should toward its mother (in our society, a qualification henceforth understood). Marsha and Marvin are unique individuals, but their relationship is only a single instance of a universal instanced by every mother and child, one token of this widespread type. Like any social relationship, the mother-child relationship is a moral fact: an observer will be able to decipher Marsha and Marvin's behavior only if he understands how they themselves think they should behave or what are the norms governing their conduct. (Sometimes we reserve "conduct" for "behavior in the consciousness of a moral norm.")

We began by asserting that a social relationship must be either primary or secondary. We amended this assertion almost immediately, recognizing instead that every nameable relationship will have both primary and secondary sides to it. The fact that it is comical to think of little Marvin leaving Marsha for another mother who offers a better deal suggests that the primary side of a relationship will be its implications for the individual's long-run capacity as a sustainer of relationships, in other words, for his moral character. (Surely the mother-child relationship is as long-lasting as any.) What is for sale is duplicatable, replaceable, but the seller himself is not. He is, as we say, a unique, unduplicatable, irreplaceable, one-of-a-kind individual. He is entitled to bargain for his advantage, but only provided the bargain reflects honor on the self which is advantaged. Primary relationships, then, or the primary sides of relationships, are those that affect that moral being, the self.

Prostitution is said to be morally wrong. If Marsha has sexual intercourse with John for fifty dollars, she will be thought to have violated the rules for distinguishing what is impersonal and for sale from what should be personal and not for sale at any price. Imagine, then, the following dialogue (the inner thoughts of the parties are supplied in brackets):

John (telephoning): "Marsha? This is John. I have two tickets to the concert—Moth Eaton and the Larvae—Saturday night. Will you come? We can go to dinner first at the Flaring Steak Pit." [This will cost an arm and a leg, but Marsha turns me on and we will go to my place afterwards.]

Marsha: "Gee, John . . . [He isn't going to put out that kind of money without expecting me to put out in return. But . . . Moth Eaton and the Flaring Steak Pit!] . . . I'd love to!"

If, however, John should add, "That's great, Marsha! Tell you what, I'll also give you fifty bucks," then Marsha will be irretrievably offended and John will be left to seek companionship elsewhere.

Imagine, now, the following dialogue:

Sidney (who has just changed dentists on *John's* advice): "You know, John, that guy has got to be the most insulting s.o.b. I ever met."

John (chuckling): "The manners of a hog, but the hands of an artist! Just keep your cool, Sidney; he's a great dentist."

Marsha feels justified in making with John what has been described as, underneath the surface appearances, really a deal for her sexual favors. She feels justified, but only so long as John assists her in sustaining the fiction that a deal is not what the relationship involves. Sidney finds his new den-

21

tist insulting, personally obnoxious, but John reminds him that his person is not at issue in his relationship to his dentist, but his teeth. Thus if someone says, "Sidney, you are the kind of guy who lets dentists insult him," Sidney can reply, "But only for a fee!" and get away with it.

Through his conduct, the individual creates an image of himself in the eyes of others and in his own eyes as well. With the distinction of primary from secondary relationships, we begin to separate the ceremonial, image-making function of the individual's conduct from its substantive utility for him. The individual designs his actions not only to promote his survival but also to portray what is to survive, himself. One may argue that the most fundamental ceremonial imperative of modern egalitarian American society requires each of us to portray himself as a unique, unduplicatable, irreplaceable, one-of-a-kind individual, and to employ the primary-secondary distinction so as to support this portrayal. In Part II, we shall be more closely concerned with the distinction of the substantive from the ceremonial components of conduct, also with the ontological status of the individuality (or selfhood, to say the same) that we portray through the latter. We shall find that the rhetoric of romantic love plays an important part in these portrayals.

§*4.2 Self-Claims and Tacit Communication*   An old romantic tradition of self-sacrifice, fidelity unto death, and other imprudent behaviors underscores the fact that we find it distasteful to think of love as contractual. The contract metaphor suggests that a loving relationship is a self-interested exchange of economic goods rather than an unselfish exchange of moral goods, goods that are essentially identical to the exchangers themselves. We introduced the distinction of primary from secondary social relationships in order to articulate this misgiving. We saw that this distinction requires the individual to portray himself as a unique being with a self, a sacred core of pride or honor not for sale at any price. In this section, we begin our examination of how these self-claims are made.

An even older skeptical tradition in philosophy obliges us to ask whether there really is such a thing as the moral self, just as we ask whether there really is such a feeling as love. Our first concern, however, must be with these questions themselves, for what they ask is far from obvious. Here we know that everyday life should be our starting point. Whether or not love and the self really do exist—and whatever it might mean for them to do so—it is a fact that we Americans say they exist and act as if they were real. We use these concepts to manage our human affairs—living and dying, marrying and divorcing, forming friendships and dissolving them. Here are the objective data on which our investigation must be based. We begin by asking how these concepts enter into our speech and action, and why they do so. Later we shall see how settling these linguistic and (as will prove to be the case) sociological questions will suggest how to settle the ontological questions that are our ultimate concern.

No doubt Robert Walpole's famous assertion, "Every man has his price," was intended to shock. (It certainly shocked Kant.)[6] Is it true? How could one possibly decide? What we do know for sure is that every man claims that ultimately or in the end or appearances to the contrary notwithstanding, he himself is not for sale. We can ask how and why persons make such claims without also asking whether or not what they claim is true. Such claims are what we may call—following Goffman, who in turn follows Durkheim and Radcliffe-Brown—ceremonial or image-making communications.[7] These communications constitute a subject-matter as determinate and factual as any theorist might wish for.

Descartes argued that the assurance each of us has of his own existence is superior in certainty to his assurance of the existence of anyone else. Other persons are inessential to one's self-consciousness, and one might therefore be the only person who exists. Such a thesis is called "solipsism."

We may begin our discussion of identity claims or assertions of selfhood by noting that whether or not the solipsist's thesis is defensible as a philosophical theory, as a recipe for everyday living, we call it madness. Identities or selves are functional in interactions. Who one is determines how one should be treated, what should be one's share of the available attention, who should defer to one, and to whom one should oneself defer. Hence persons can interact intelligibly only on the basis of an agreement or consensus about who each of them is. The cliché lunatic who claims to be Napoleon imposes impossible identity requirements on those who would interact with him as if he were sane. If they agree with him, then others will not agree with them, and their own identities are put at risk. Hence they think him mad.

For our purposes, and at this stage of the argument, the existence of the institution of insanity or "mental illness" may be taken to be a sufficient refutation of solipsism. (Later we shall confront the philosophical skeptic directly.) Other persons, then, are essential to the individual's self-consciousness: his very being requires his being known to others. Precisely this is implied, in fact, by the concept of socialization introduced in §3. The self each of us has is the self he was taught to have, so that when one learns one's name, one also learns who that name stands for.

A dialectical conclusion follows immediately: the purpose of portraying himself as a unique individual with a sacred inner integrity cannot, save derivatively, be a purpose willed by the individual himself, for he himself can be said to exist only in so far as that purpose is already achieved. In other words, the individual may aspire to a better or more advantageous identity, but not to an identity in the first place, for until he has one, there exists no one to do the aspiring.

The principle underlying this conclusion is called "functionalism." This is the principle that the agency which ultimately authorizes identities, namely society, exists only through its members, persons, and therefore maintains its existence across time by continually creating new persons. It creates them by socializing them, transforming what begin as adorable but formless blobs of infant protoplasm into articulate adults who know their names and their rights and who know how to protest when their rights are infringed upon. According to this principle, then, the individual's existence is fundamentally a realization of society's collective purpose of self-maintenance, and only derivatively a purpose of the individual himself.

Our general aim is to present and defend a set of philosophical principles of explanation by showing those principles actually at work. We use them to construct a theory at once of love and of the question, "What is love?" The test of the principles is to be their ability to explain this apparently inexplicable phenomenon and to answer this questionable question. We know that we seek an ontological answer, an answer that establishes what kind of being love has.

In keeping with this general aim, we introduce explanatory principles into the argument only where the argument itself comes to require them, that is, only where we need them to explain love. Defending these principles involves delicate issues of argumentative strategy. In one sense—surely the most important—the "defense" of a principle of explanation is simply the principle's power to explain. For that defense, the principle must be permitted to display its power. In addition, however, explanatory principles entail ontological commitments, commitments that may seem uncongenial on other grounds, and in this secondary sense, a principle may require an independent defense.

Functionalism clearly requires such an independent defense. From §4.1 we assume that the imperative of distinguishing primary from secondary relationships, dignity from price, or moral values from economic values is fundamental to the modern American society of which we are all members. We are required to present ourselves to one another as if we possessed moral selves, the "moral self" being the individual's portrayal of himself as a long-term sustainer of relationships, in other words, as someone competent to employ the same distinction between the moral and the economic that requires the portrayal. The individual, so conceived, is the activity of claiming a correct, long-term alignment to the prevailing moral values,[8] the primary-secondary distinction being chief among them. Those values, then, might be said to be what authorizes identities, for only by being referred to them may a self be convincingly claimed. To speak of them,

24

however—as functionalism requires us to speak—as if they were a collective agency with a being of its own, appears to be an ontologically dubious *façon de parler*, at odds with the individualism and nominalism traditional in Anglo-American philosophy. Is there really such a *thing* as society, or is "society" merely a convenient, shorthand way of referring to the independent, presumably natural existence of many individuals? Certainly the explanatory principles available to us at this stage in the argument are incapable of solving this problem, or even of clarifying it. We shall return to it, better equipped, in Part III.

Granted—as it were, on sufferance—the functionalism implied by the primary-secondary distinction, here we may proceed to examine certain elementary principles of social interaction. We restrict our examination to two-person interactions, though this restriction could easily be removed. Two persons may be said to "interact" when each modifies his actions by what he perceives to be the actions of the other. Interactions may be "direct" or "face to face," on the one hand, or "indirect" on the other. In face-to-face interaction, participants are within easy earshot and eyeshot, so that each can respond promptly to the other's words and actions. Face-to-face interactions or "encounters" feature, as Goffman puts it, "richness of information flow" and "facilitation of feedback."[9] In indirect interaction, by contrast, time and space separate the sending of a message from the receiving of it. Therefore the message makes directly available to the receiver only its explicit verbal content and not also the sender's behavioral context at the time of transmission. Lovers' meetings are face-to-face interactions. Exchanges of letters are indirect. Telephone calls are ambiguous. Although we find the distinction sometimes ambiguous in application, it is nevertheless fundamental to the morality of interaction. Face-to-face interactions, interactions "in person," function as the test of identities privately fantasized or indirectly claimed. I may think to myself that I have a pleasing baritone voice, but if others flee when I open my mouth to sing, then I shall have to change my self-image. John may court Marsha by mail, but this epistolary relationship is only a potential romance until they actually meet. Thus the self one really possesses is the self one can use in face-to-face interaction with others: their agreement is required for one to be oneself. And this dependency is reciprocal, for the same is true of each of them.

Accordingly, communications about oneself can always be construed as negotiations. When two persons commence face-to-face interaction, whatever either may explicitly say about himself during the interaction must rest upon what the other has implicitly conceded at the beginning, for before one can speak, one must have an identity to speak from. Explicit exchanging of information about self thus presupposes tacit agreement about who is talking. Such an agreement may be explicitly renegotiated—"Oh, excuse me, you look so young, are you a faculty member?''—but not explicitly negotiated. When persons come into one another's presence, they tacitly or wordlessly size one another up, take one another's measure, scrutinize one another's appearance and manner for clues to what line to follow during the subsequent interaction. Such fundamental identifiers as age, sex, and social class are gleaned from facial expression, dress, posture, location (the bar as opposed to the library), company (the fast crowd rather than the Stamp Club), and a host of other signs. These "signals given off" are used to establish the identity from which whatever each speaker says will be presumed to issue. Explicit messages—"signals given"—thus presuppose what is implicitly communicated through "signals given off," through tacit physical and behavioral clues.[10]

The distinction between signals given and signals given off might be said to be a distinction between two different channels of communication, the first transmitting information about the speaker through explicit verbal assertions, the second transmitting information about him through opportunities to make inferences about him. The distinction between tacit and explicit communication, on the other hand, is a distinction in logical function between communication establishing the *persona* or identity of the speaker and communication issuing from him in that identity—the behavioral analogue of the literary distinction between style and content.

Although image-forming or identity-establishing information will in general be conveyed through the signals-given-off channel and explicit self-claims through the signals-given or overt utterance channel, this pairing does not always obtain. Wearing a uniform is a behavioral way of making an explicit self-claim, and explicit utterances themselves will be read for such implicit clues to the speaker's identity as style and accent. Explicit verbal self-claims can be made with little physical effort and are often easily changed or withdrawn. By contrast, claims implicitly made by giving off signals through appearance, behavior, setting, and the like tend to be longer-lasting and harder to manipulate. Others will therefore use them as a check on signals given. Someone who presents a meek and humble appearance but says of himself that he is bold and dashing will raise questions in the minds of his interactants that he would not have raised had his explicit and implicit self-claims been more in harmony. Behind the interplay between the two, implicit communication enjoys absolute priority, since explicit speech must issue from a speaker.

When we apply the distinction between implicit, identity-establishing communication and the explicit communication that presupposes it to contractual relationships between persons, then clearly business contracts and in general secondary relationships will be fitting matters for explicit formulation and open negotiation, for here the parties deal with duplicatable, dispensable goods such as money. Such primary relationships as friendships and romances will not be fitting matters, however, for here the goods exchanged are held to be identical with the parties exchanging them. These latter negotiations are therefore especially risky. Should John offer to sell his car to Sidney for five hundred dollars, he runs a risk in the offer, for Sidney or someone else might be willing to pay more. When John offers his friendship to Sidney, however, he puts himself far more gravely at risk. "John's friendship" is really another name for John himself. It is supposed to be desirable for its own sake, just as John himself is supposed to be desirable for his own sake. Sidney's spurning it threatens John's ability to conceive of himself as intrinsically worthy. That ability is John's very self. The more openly he offers himself to Sidney, the more difficult it will be for him to repair the damage done by a refusal.

Therefore negotiations over primary relationships must be fundamentally tacit. Through this tacitness, negotiators minimize the risks to themselves. This hedging is not optional, since primary relationships are held to be to some extent constitutive of their relata. Thus when John says, "I just can't help loving Marsha" (an idiom to which we shall return), we may translate, "It is not as if I, John, possessed an identity independently of my affection for Marsha and then saw that affection to be advantageous to me; rather I and my affection for Marsha are one." He may not mean this; he may be insincere or self-deluded. But this is what he *says*, and what we understand him to have said.

In this section, we have examined some of the elementary principles of social interaction. Principles such as that the self one really possesses is the self one can use in face-to-face interaction, that explicit self-claims rest on implicit, and that primary relationships must be tacitly negotiated in order to minimize risks, were said to be "necessary." One might well ask what "necessary" means here, since the principles examined seem hard to classify as straightforwardly psychological, moral, or prudential.

One way to think of them is as logical principles. Thus one may argue that interaction, like action, has its logical form. In order to speak intelligibly or act effectively, the individual must refrain from contradicting himself. Here is a familiar fundamental law of logic, which, because it is a fundamental law of logic, cannot be proved, but only pointed out in more or less sophisticated ways. But then what is necessary for one is also necessary for two or more: logical principles on a par with the principle of non-contradiction distinguish meaningful from meaningless interactions, and the most fundamental of these principles cannot be proved, but only more or less artfully pointed out. The sense our interactions make depends, of course, on certain contingencies, psychological facts, and contemporary morals. But we use familiar logical principles to appraise the equally contingent content of individual actions and utterances. The distinction between meaningful and meaningless conversation and cooperation is more complicated, for participants in an interaction must both understand one another and understand one another's understanding of one another. This requirement generates the indefinite regress made famous by George H. Mead, and a logic whose principles define the consistency of message, sender, and receiver taken together as a unit. Such a complex distinction makes a logic that is difficult to formulate accurately, but a logic that is nevertheless an extension of the more familiar logic of individual statements and actions.

§4.3 The Moral Order and the Legal Order A metaphor compares a thing with something else that resembles it in some ways but differs from it in others, the intention of the metaphor being to call attention to the resemblances. We have proceeded on the assumption that we find it distasteful to compare romances to contractual relationships, for we think this metaphor obscures morally essential differences between the two. Parties to a legal contract have a secondary or economic relationship, while lovers have a primary or moral relationship. We examined this distinction in §4.2.

A contract is a legal instrument, defined by legislation and enforceable by the courts. A romance, by contrast, is a moral relationship. Romantic love bears a special relationship to the legal, contractual institution of marriage (and to the religious sacrament of marriage). This relationship is an instance of a more general relationship of morals to the law. The contract metaphor disturbs us, it would seem, because we feel that morality and the law should be kept distinct. This feeling is revealed by such commonplace sayings as "You can't legislate morality" and "Everyone has his own morals." Moreover, in so far as the law is explicit and public while morals are (or at least are said to be) private and tacit, this third distinction incorporates the first two.

Our purpose is to produce a theory at once of love and of the question, "What is love?" Love is a topic on which the layman uneasily vacillates between the feeling that here, as everywhere else in modern life, there should be experts to tell him what to think and how to feel, and the conviction that no matter what any expert may say, his own heart of hearts is his only reliable guide. Therefore "What is love?" is said to be at best a supremely difficult question, at worst an utterly unanswerable one.

When a question is said to be difficult or impossible to answer, however, we can always ask why. "Difficult" and "impossible" are contrast words. A question is "difficult" in contrast to other questions of the same sort which are not so difficult. Questions about the future, for example, are often difficult in contrast to questions about the past or the present, for the future has not happened yet. Or questions about a great many intricate things are often difficult in contrast to questions about a few simple things, for human attention span and memory are limited. We began by supposing that love is a feeling. On that supposition, "What is love?" will be a difficult question because feelings are concrete and descriptions necessarily abstract. Here feelings are implicitly contrasted with policies and contracts, both of which can be abstractly formulated. Then we saw that love can be a feeling only by also being a contractual relationship. It should be possible, therefore, to say what love is. We need only describe the terms of lovers' contracts, specifying the goods exchanged and the conditions of exchange, distinguishing ideals or standards from typical actual contracts. These contracts are supposed to be in general tacitly understood rather than overtly expressed. Therefore a veil of moral resistances will hide their contents from us, and the question will still be difficult. We shall have to fall back upon social-scientific techniques for interpreting behavior objectively. But we will be able to answer the question, for any exchange relationship must be analyzable, whether the goods exchanged be economic, moral, or psychological.

We have assumed that this line of inquiry and the contractual conception of love on which it is based are distasteful. In the last two sections, we have tried to articulate this distaste. Our results so far seem inconclusive. "What is love?" remains unanswered, and it is not yet clear how we should proceed. Questions about legal relationships (especially "What is marriage?") offer one possible comparison to "What is love?" but a comparison whose significance is still obscure. We are entitled to suspect that the answer to our question, or at any rate a clearer formulation of it, may lie in the general relationship of morals to law, and hence we should explore that relationship in this section.

The Greeks thought the primary function of the law was the education of citizens.[11] They regarded the regulatory function of law as secondary. We, on the other hand, derive our conceptions of law and government from the social-contract theorists of the Enlightenment, Locke, Montesquieu, and Jefferson, and we separate church from state. Therefore we tend to invert the Greek view. We say, "You can't legislate morality," and we think that while civil and criminal law are public, "Everyone has his own morals," his own private version of moral law. Alongside a vague awareness that the law depends for its authority on its moral legitimacy, we feel an obligation to make a clear and sharp distinction between morals and the law.

The law, so this sharp distinction runs, is made public by being codified, written down, published at public expense. Morals, by contrast, are tacit and private. The law is enforced by sanctions. Violators risk physical and financial punishment. Morals, by contrast, are enforced only by the internal sanctions of conscience. The law enjoins observable actions, but morality enjoins the internal compliance of good intentions. The law is satisfied if the individual does what it commands; whether he does so out of fear, joy, or duty is immaterial. Morality, however, commands that the individual do his duty simply because it is his duty and without regard for how this entirely internal transaction between himself and his conscience may appear to others when externalized in the form of action.

If we look more closely, however, this sharp distinction begins to blur. Moral standards are said to be private, but we use them to criticize one another. Indeed, a standard is universal by its very nature as a standard: it applies to every relevant case, and if a statement of it proves to have exceptions, that proves the statement inaccurate. We say that the individual's conscience alone enforces the moral law, but we delight in one another's praise and we dislike being blamed. And the sanctions internal in conscience begin by being external. It may be that children are naturally conscientious—at least the thought is a pleasant one—but they must still be taught how to be conscientious, sometimes by physical punishment. The law resides in an institutional apparatus of courts, police, and prisons, but morality too has its institutional loci in schools, churches, and censorship boards.

What we took to be the most prominent feature distinguishing morality from the law, namely its privacy, its dependence upon the individual's conscience, seems the more dubious the more closely one examines it. Morality resides in the individual's conscience, to be sure, but only because society put it there. To say that morality and moral relationships such as love owe their collective significance and common authority to the spontaneous coincidence of individual consciences ignores the evidence that our moral conceptions owe their uniformity to the same well-known social processes that produce our common conception of the law.

So far, we have examined morality only in contrast to law. We should examine it in itself. Sometimes, as a residue of our puritan heritage, we associate "morals" with harsh restraints and "good morals" with a narrow and hypocritical abstemiousness. Here we take a most moralistic attitude toward morality: evidently the topic can be considered with different degrees of insight and sophistication. What we say and what we really think do not always coincide, providing an opportunity for the expert to probe beneath the surface appearances. The standard ethicist's definition of morality is drawn from the Greeks, who distinguished an action done for the sake of the action itself from an action done for the sake of consequences lying beyond it. One buys a coat in order to keep warm and visits the doctor in order to preserve one's health, but one acts virtuously simply in order to act virtuously—or else the action is not really virtuous. By definition, then, an action is "moral" when or in so far as the end of the action lies in the action itself, and ethics, morals, or practical philosophy—terms we shall treat as synonyms—concern actions of this sort or, said differently, concern this dimension of action.

One might well ask why morality so defined should be thought to depend especially upon the individual as such. One plausible answer is this: Suppose that, as a second approximation (the first is in §3), we define "society" as a moral order—thus as an order that exists for its own sake—that has the power to realize itself in the form of socialized persons. "Socialized person" is a tautology. The newborn infant is a bundle of random impulses and unrealized capacities. He matures as parents and community mold his actions and beliefs, training him to contain his bodily fluids, to restrain his aggressions, to temper and schedule his moods, in general training him to render himself intelligible and convenient to others. We may infer how adults are expected to be trained by considering the behaviors we tolerate only in small children. The two-year-old, for example, may have to be told not to bite his playmates. Adults are expected to have formed the habit of not biting others, and the adult who is perceived as having consciously to restrain himself from biting will be thought quite literally mad. One learns to drive an automobile by internalizing abstract instructions—"Let up on the gas pedal when you approach a turn"—converting those instructions into unthinking, automatic responses, so that the practiced driver would find it very difficult to articulate all he does. Socialization is a similar process of internalization or habituation, although less explicitly verbal, more extensive, and infinitely riskier. Thus the socialization process becomes visible against the counterfoil of the mentally ill, who are often guilty of offenses tolerated in small children—biting, drooling, incontinence, and the like—and who are therefore removed altogether from the moral order.[12] Someone certified insane has lost that index of moral credibility, the power to insult, for whatever he says may be discounted as symptomatic.

Aristotle maintained that virtues are habits. We too ought to view the sane adult as the locus of a set of good habits. Those good habits tend not to be noticed, for they are primarily negative: he does not bite others, drool, befoul himself, suddenly break out in uncontrollable rage, and so on. In Goffman's words, he is properly "deferential" to others and "well-demeaned" in himself; he fits into the social situations in which he finds himself.[13] This self-restraint is not painful to him. In fact, were he to sense himself losing it—as an accompaniment of the onset of mental disease—he would find the experience shattering.[14] He is not conscious of these manifold negative actions or nondoings. Indeed, he passes among others as sane and responsible by unceasingly communicating this unconsciousness to others through tacit behavioral clues, through signals given off. The positive purpose of these negative actions is the portrayal they implicitly convey of others as unique, infinitely worthy beings like himself, beings whose sensitivities (he insinuates) he respects and whose rights he honors. Reciprocally, the portrayal is of course also a portrayal of himself as sane and responsible. His actions are thus a constant attestation to the legitimacy of the moral order which created him and to which he owes his existence as a person.

From this functionalistic point of view, rather than thinking of morals as harsh restraints, we shall find useful the contrary principle of associating "moral" with what we find natural, easeful, tasteful, and enjoyable. As a general rule, what we like to do is what we have been trained to do, and as a general rule, what we have been trained to do is what we think we ought to do. Our actual ideals can therefore often be roughly inferred from our preferences.

The moral order—society—realizes itself by concealing itself from its creatures, persons. It conceals itself in their habits of attention and enjoyment, in what they are sensitive to, and in how they distribute emphasis. However, as the existence of the mentally ill (among others) testifies, society does not always succeed in realizing itself. Like nature, it too has its slips, mistakes, failures, and abortions. Corrective apparatus is therefore necessary. External social or moral controls—negative feedback pressures from others—usually operate tacitly or unconsciously, but must now and then cross the threshold of consciousness and become explicit. But we ought to look upon this apparatus of conscious correction as a secondary, derivative feature of the moral order. As a rule, among adults when a problem has reached the stage where "You should not do that" must be said, processes which should have operated silently and automatically have failed, the need for an open reproof being token of the failure. The failure has become not merely the moral failure of some individual, but also— what is far more serious—a local, temporary failure of the moral order itself. (For this reason, it may be argued, ethical theories that base themselves entirely on our explicit uses of the vocabulary of moral assessment and correction, on the grammar of terms such as "good," "bad," "right," "wrong," "just," and "unjust," commit a methodological error, much as if one tried to derive an account of the automobile in our culture from police accident reports.)

The individual thinks the moral order depends upon the spontaneity of his individual conscience because he has been trained to obey the moral law spontaneously, habitually. In other words, he has been trained to have a conscience, but not to notice where his conscience came from. There may be good reasons for his obligations, but he should seldom need to reason about them. After all, if very many moral actions required prior deliberation, social life would immediately stall. Far better, then, that we should do our duty spontaneously, without noticing what we are doing and without needing to remember why we do it. In this regard, moral training differs from other forms of training only in its scope and seriousness.

On rare occasions, the automatism of habit proves undependable. Then the moral order falls back upon explicit social controls. These first take the form of reasonable pleadings, warnings, rebukes. On those still rarer occasions when these gentle methods fail, then morality crystallizes into the forceful machinery of the law. Thus the legal order functions as a backstop for the moral order, rightfully enforcing the civil peace which makes morality possible.

Regarded in this way, the contrast between morality and the law is a contrast between one part of the moral order and another—between the smooth, silent, automatic functioning of moral controls to which we are trained to aspire and the harsh justice which must now and then support it. The contrast is understandably not sharp, for it involves contrasting a thing with itself. We insist that it is sharp as a way of implying that we are trustworthy persons who will do what we are supposed to do without needing to be threatened. We say, "Everyone has his own morals," tacitly adding "provided his morals are the same as everyone else's," and when we encounter someone with genuinely different morals, we think him mad. We say, "You can't legislate morality," but in fact you cannot legislate anything else except morality, for the law owes its authority to its legitimacy, and owes its legitimacy to the moral order that created it.

The relation of romantic love to marriage exemplifies this general conception of the relation of morals to the law. Both love and marriage are contractual exchanges. If everyone could always be trusted to do the right thing, then the tacit warmth of love would suffice to perpetuate the moral order. Persons in or out of love are sometimes untrustworthy, however, threatening not only one another but also such innocent third parties as the children they have produced. Therefore society employs explicit laws and forceful penalties to keep their behavior within reasonable bounds.

What, then, is love? A primary, fundamentally tacit, contractual relationship between persons who may become sexually involved with one another. Like marriage, love is an exchange relationship, and from the minimum decencies we enforce through the marriage laws, we can extrapolate the unexpressed ideals that define lovers' contracts, determining what is exchanged, on what terms, and so forth. Such an analysis should show the relation of the interdependent institutions of love and marriage to other social institutions: for example, the extended family, the class structure, and the institution of work. Both the evidence on which it would be based and the generalizations it would produce are sociological: it would be a functionalistic analysis. The rules that define love are moral rules, rules of conduct, but for that very reason, only the sociological expert can produce an accurate analysis of them. The layman is trained to live by them, not to think about them—indeed, to *not* think about them. He lacks the discipline of objectivity. Therefore, so we may argue, an analysis of love not only is beyond the layman's powers, but even should be beyond the layman's powers; for were it not so, lay reflections would spoil the state of habitual grace necessary for the smooth functioning of social life.

Although this argument seems plausible enough to be worth pursuing in some detail, it is open to a puzzling and serious objection. We may readily grant that love is a social institution. Therefore it ought to be analyzed by the same method as any other social institution. The result would be an empirical theory of love that claims the same objectivity as any other social-scientific theory. Nevertheless, the layman does think that everyone has his own morals, that you cannot legislate morality, and that no one can say what love is. We have anticipated that our sociological theory will show that these lay opinions are false, and why, just as lay opinions about such scientifically esoteric matters as the structure of the atom and the causes of cancer are for the most part false. Physicists and medical researchers, however, base their theories upon special experiences in the laboratory and clinic, experiences the layman has not had; they do not base their theories upon their own experiences as laymen. Their experts' experiences entitle them to theories that contradict lay opinion. Our sociological theory, however, will be based upon experience of the same society, the same moral order that legitimates physics, medicine, and sociology. This moral experience is therefore logically prior to the special experiences of experts (a point we shall consider in detail later), and is in principle equally accessible to everyone.

We should bear in mind that if we argue that the sociologist is right and the layman wrong about what love is, we argue with a tacit qualification, namely that the sociologist is right to another sociologist, as one expert to another. What the sociologist claims to be right about, however, are the intimate experiences of the layman, experiences the layman alone is entitled to define. Those experiences are accessible to the sociologist only in his prior capacity as layman. To the objection—heralded in light fiction, the movies, and the like as crushing—that theorizing about love ruins one's ability to experience it, the best rejoinder would be a theory of love acceptable to the layman himself. Thus it will not do to say that the theoretically defined reality of love contradicts how love appears to the layman, for love after all is an appearance, an immediate experience, something that seems to happen—to the layman. What is at issue here is the expert's right to theorize about moral reality and about love as its most prominent feature, and this issue appears to be neither straightforwardly theoretical nor straightforwardly moral.

In Part II, we shall construct and evaluate a functionalistic, sociological theory of romantic love. We do so with the twofold purpose of constructing the theory and determining the theoretical legitimacy of this theorizing. In the first purpose, we are concerned with what love is; in the second, with the question, "What is love?" As we noted just above, a theory of love also poses the puzzling problem of the moral legitimacy of such a theory, a problem difficult to classify. We shall examine it in Part III.

Part II
The Social Function of Love

§5 Functionalism

Philosophy is the study of questions as such. In our view, therefore, the discipline ought to study messy and troublesome questions rather than neat and straightforward ones, for while the latter call for answers, the former raise in fresh and fruitful ways such second-order questions as "What is a question?" and "What is an explanation?" Straightforward questions are products of philosophical inquiry, but messy questions are invitations to engage in it.

The messy question we study in this book is "What is love?" Our concern with this question is ontological, that is, we want to discover what love is "really." After the preliminary methodological remarks of the Introduction, we examined in §3 the most trite and familiar answer: love is a certain feeling. We argued that since in everyday life we take feelings to be tested by policies and policies by contracts, love is more accurately described as a contractual relationship. In §4 and its subsections we examined this description. At this point in the argument, our conclusion is that romantic love is a primary, fundamentally tacit, contractual relationship between persons who may become sexually involved with one another. Such a relationship will be manifested through certain feelings, of course, but what each party actually contracts to is a policy, a long-term commitment to a pattern of action.

Given our ontological concern, this answer is—perhaps rather obviously—incomplete; and even while arriving at it, we entertained several misgivings. Moreover, we arrived at it in a less than systematic way. We plunged directly into answering "What is love?" without first establishing what should count as an answer. This relaxed procedure is philosophically sensible, for to declare at the outset what shall count as explaining love would surely be dogmatic. While we are interested in what love really is, we have a deeper interest in determining what to make of the question "What is love?" and an even deeper interest in developing a philosophical theory of explanation from this determination. Therefore we plunged directly into our subject-matter, love, with the thought that our sense for the question and our principles of explanation ought to emerge from that subject-matter itself, emerging together with our felt need for them. Such a procedure provides some guarantee of the significance of our principles, some small assurance that our philosophical abstractions are really abstracted from everyday life rather than merely imposed upon it.

We began by classifying love as a feeling. Here we are accustomed to assuming that psychological explanations are appropriate. When we looked for this feeling, we found it, of course, but we also found policies, contracts, moral rules, and an apparently essential overlay of rhetoric and ceremonial. These latter seem to require more than strictly psychological explanation. Here we might have turned to philosophy—to normative ethics—but instead we began to employ sociological principles and distinctions. Thus the argument depended on a disciplinary division of labor which we never examined or justified. In this section, we must remedy this omission and justify the sociological excursion that occupies most of Part II. We shall also take a first look at philosophical skepticism.

A discipline may be thought of as a tradition of explaining. Some traditions are older, some younger. Western philosophy, for example, begins with Thales, who is said to have predicted an eclipse of the sun in 585 B.C. Psychology and sociology are much younger, both Freud (1856–1939) and Durkheim (1858–1917) having been active in the early decades of this century. This conception of a discipline as a tradition of explaining provides a definition of "fact" that we shall find useful. Thus even though disciplinary boundaries are occasionally vague or merely conventional, nevertheless we may think of a "fact" as the product of a disciplinary tradition. A fact is what one could explain if asked, "Why do you claim it's a fact that . . . ?" or "Why do you say that . . . ?" There are in this sense as many kinds of fact as there are disciplines: facts of physics, geology, art history, and so on. If, then, someone should assert that it is a fact that people fall in love, we are entitled to ask why he asserts this, what are his grounds for the assertion, and what disciplinary tradition guarantees the relevance of those grounds to that assertion. Defining "fact" in this way is useful for the shift of emphasis implied: where we began by groping for information about obscure and difficult facts, now we can try to see the confluence and divergence of different traditions of explaining.

We began with a fact, the feeling of love, that is said to be amenable to psychological explanation. But what counts as a psychological explanation? Although the question is certainly controversial, setting aside social psychology (for our purposes, a separate discipline), perhaps it will be neutral enough to define psychology as the empirical study of individual behavior. The explanatory unit of psychology, then, is the individual organism. It is alive and it tries to preserve its life—that much is implied by "organism." We assume evolution has provided it with drives whose satisfaction tends to preserve its life and with physical and mental equipment well adapted for satisfying those drives. Given this explanatory unit, the psychologist observes and experiments in order to discover laws of individual behavior. The aim and the test of this theorizing is successful prediction.

The organism receives informational input from its environment and transforms this input into behavioral output. The significance of the environment to the organism—in other words, what will count as input—is determined by the organism's drives. Input is transformed into behavioral output that is in general well designed to reduce the drives. What the psychologist aims to discover, then, are laws of the organism's transformation mechanisms, laws that will enable him, for a given state of environment and drives, to predict behavioral output.

We may ask what are the limits of this form of explanation. What, if anything, cannot these principles explain about human behavior? Certainly we can say this: we mean a drive to be satisfiable by something that can be described entirely in general terms. Thirst is a drive for water—any water; hunger, a drive for food—any food. The sexual urge is a drive for sexual gratification—from any source. (The last example is, of course, maliciously chosen.) A natural drive is satisfiable by anything of the proper kind, not by some particular individual thing only.

Romantic love, however, as we noted in §3, is a social feeling or "particularistic emotion," a feeling whose object is not anything of a certain kind, but some particular individual. Persons are supposed to fall in love with one another as individuals. If we ask for the mechanism underlying such a social feeling, the most psychology can provide will be a need analysis, an explanation in terms of drives for affection and companionship. When Marsha falls in love with John, however, she claims that what she wants is John—John himself, in the flesh, as it were—not any male of a John-like kind. She wants a primary relationship, and primary relationships are supposed to relate individuals as such. "Oh, God, how I need John!" may express love, but "Oh, God, how I need a man!" will be interpreted as an expression of sexual frustration. One familiar way of insulting a person by attributing to him a subhuman, animal mentality is to submit his primary relationships to a need analysis. Thus Uncle Tom weeps at leaving Aunt Chloe, but only a Simon Legree would think it comforting to tell him there will be women at his next plantation too.

What we say about love and the other primary relationships appears to resist explanation in psychological terms. Since, she declares, only John will satisfy Marsha's yearning, we cannot account for the difference between requited and unrequited love by talking merely about the organism and its drives. We shifted, therefore, from defining love as a feeling to defining it as a contractual relationship.

The disciplinary implications of this contractual definition seem ethical. Although we say that feelings can be either fostered and cultivated or controlled and repressed, nevertheless fundamentally "a feeling" refers to a passivity, to something that happens to one, in contrast to something one does. A contract, on the other hand, is a mutual promise, and a promise, like a policy, is an ethical action. Given, then, that romantic relationships are contractual; that contracts are promises; promises, ways of conducting oneself; and conduct, behavior in the consciousness of moral norms—behavior, therefore, on which we feel entitled to pass moral judgment—"What is love?" becomes a problem in ethics. The individual who asks what love really is wants to know what are the rules governing this contractual relationship and how those rules are related to the rules governing other primary relationships. Some of those rules may be obvious (for example, the incest taboos), but many of them are not; relationships often conflict, and in any case good judgment is required for fitting general rules to particular situations. The perplexed layman will be well advised, therefore, to seek expert advice—at its best, advice from the ethical philosopher.

We said in §4.3 that the moral order is "hidden," hidden in the sense that individuals—laymen—are normally required to act spontaneously, habitually. Their duty is not to question society's rules, but rather to act upon them. Sometimes this spontaneity is neither possible nor ethically desirable. For example, the layman who asks what love really is typically finds himself torn between conflicting duties, caught up in a jurisdictional dispute among moral rules. Although none of us chose those rules, having rather inherited them, nevertheless from time to time it becomes the duty of a conscientious person to review them as if he were choosing them. The ethical philosopher undertakes to be expert at this activity, at justifying an order among obligations, settling jurisdictional disputes, resolving ambiguities. He, then, if anyone, can provide the layman with good reasons for honoring one obligation over another—reasons "good" in the sense that the layman can convince himself that they are good. If love really is a set of moral rules governing certain contractual relationships, then explaining those rules will mean showing where they stand among all our moral rules, establishing the limits of love's moral authority. A moral order creates reasons that function in accounts, apologies, excuses, justifications, and pretexts. What love really is is determined by which actions love really justifies, and on this question, the ethical philosopher is the relevant expert.

II. The Social Function of Love

Love is a complicated affair, to be sure. But suppose the ethical philosopher had done his very best, providing us a complete and completely persuasive explanation of our moral rules for romancing, an explanation (which would also be a justification) establishing in detail where those rules prevail and where other rules override them. Here we would have an ethical answer to the question, "What is love?"

Without questioning the ethical merits of such an answer, one may question its explanatory completeness. For consider the analogy of work. In our society we have a work ethic just as we have a love ethic—two sets of obligations to which we are subject as laymen. The perplexed individual who asks what work really is wants to know what he is supposed to think and do about it; presumably the ethical philosopher can tell him. We know from sociology and social anthropology, however, that this advice will be historically relative. Attitudes toward work are a function of general social organization. They have varied widely across the centuries. Work to the ancients was a curse and to the medievals a divine punishment. Work to us is a duty to be joyfully embraced, an ethic functional for a mass-production economy.[1]

There is a clear difference between explaining obligations from within a moral system, on the one hand, and explaining that system itself—as it were, from without—on the other. In the first kind of explanation, the distinction between moral and nonmoral questions is assumed; in the second, it is explained. When the layman asks the ethical philosopher what love or work really is, this transaction is internal to our morality. The layman knows the difference between moral and nonmoral questions, knows who counts as an expert about the former and what counts as a good reason. But how we say the individual ought to manage his loves and labors is one kind of question, the ethical kind; why we define "individual," "love," and "work" as we do, on the other hand, are comparative sociological questions. The latter concern not the reasons individuals give, but the collective reasons for those individual reasons, collective reasons that become apparent only when we take the point of view of society itself, seeing our morality in contrast to others prevailing elsewhere or earlier.

Morals change. We have no reason for supposing our morals less likely to be superseded than past morals were. Romantic love in particular is a comparatively new idea that grew out of the "courtly love" invented by a handful of poets and noblemen in late eleventh-century France.[2] To be sure, the individual can no more jump out of his time than out of his skin. The contemporary individual will find the answer to "What is love?" in normative ethics. He is obliged to accept that answer, and we too shall accept it here. On the other hand, this is a local and temporary answer that can in turn be explained by contrasting our society with its rivals and predecessors. Sometimes we catch ourselves supposing that our ancestors had their strange customs and beliefs because they were too naive and uncivilized to think of better. In our better moments, however, we recognize that their world was a world, a systematic whole each of whose parts had its place and its significance, so that their mating and marriage customs, like their diet and dress, were the results not of their ignorance, but simply of the way they lived. What love really is, then, depends upon what each of us is individually required to say, think, and do about it. The meaning of this love ethic, however, depends upon the use we collectively make of it, a use that may well be hidden from the lay individual. Here our ethical beliefs become data for comparative sociology, and here we turn from local and temporary phenomena to the universal laws of social life that explain them.

Suppose we look upon our own society as a moral order endeavoring to maintain itself through time in a natural environment and under historically given conditions. A moral order realizes itself in the form of persons, human beings trained to recognize and abide by its rules. The overt, formal expression of the moral order is the legal or political order. The latter is composed of institutions—explicit, officially sanctioned ways for persons to relate to one another. Extending this notion, we may think of collective systematic habits such as romantic love as informal institutions. Society, then, sustains itself through its least units, persons, by organizing those least units into formal and informal institutions. We assume that society has the power to sustain itself—at least, to sustain itself long enough to be worth theorizing about. Granted this assumption, it follows that society's institutions, the deputies of its absolute moral authority, must be mutually supporting, must contribute to one another's contributions to their conjoint realization of the social whole. What will count, therefore, as an explanation of a given institution—such as romantic love—will be an account of how it supports society's other institutions, contributing thus to the homeostasis or sameness-through-time of the social whole. As we noted in §4.2, this principle of explanation is called "functionalism."

Functionalism has been a controversial topic in recent social science.[3] We shall examine one major strand of controversy toward the end of Part II. Our primary interest is not in sociology itself, however, but in its ontological presuppositions. The version—basic and simple—of functionalism we adopt here is drawn from the great French sociologist, Emile Durkheim. Durkheim's sociology was a reaction against the Utilitarian conception of society as the product of contractual relations among individuals, especially as that conception was developed by Herbert Spencer. The social-contract tradition is nominalistic: individuals exist primarily, groups only derivatively, universals only in language. By nature, individuals seek to preserve themselves, each pursuing his own interests. They discover that their individual interests are better served by limiting competition, so they contract with one another to cooperate in manifold ways. It follows that the elements of stability in society—institutions—are arrested and transmuted conflicts, truces in the never-ending struggle for individual power, an idea that can be traced back to Hobbes. Talcott Parsons writes:

> . . . Durkheim shows, with characteristic thoroughness and penetration, that Spencer's assumptions—which were common to the whole liberal branch of the utilitarian tradition—failed to account for even the most elementary component of order in a system of social relations that was allegedly based on the pursuit of individual self-interest. . . . As is well known, Durkheim's emphasis is on the *institution* of contract, which at one point he characterizes as consisting in the "non-contractual elements" of contract. These are not items agreed upon by contracting parties in the particular situation, but are norms established in the society, norms which underlie and are independent of any particular contract.[4]

This says, in another way, that social contract theories are circular, for they treat the moral rules that make contracts possible as if those rules resulted from contracts. Hobbes' *Leviathan* provides a clear example of this circular reasoning. Hobbes' description of the "state of nature," the absence of civil society, is famous: it is the "war, where every man is enemy to every man," and as a result, human life is "solitary, poor, nasty, brutish, and short."[5] Seeking escape from this misery, men come together and covenant with one another, conferring the right to govern them upon a sovereign. Men come together—but how? This coming together is what the social-contract theory was supposed to account for.

Durkheim was free from the nominalistic commitments underlying social-contract theories. He did not feel compelled to show that supraindividual things such as groups, institutions, and society itself are generated by the activities of individuals. Instead he felt the natural order of explanation is the reverse, from the collective reality of society to the activities and sentiments of individual men. In his first major work, *The Division of Labor in Society*, he wrote:

> The totality of beliefs and sentiments common to average citizens of the same society forms a determinate system which has its own life; one may call it the *collective* or *common conscience*. No doubt it has not a specific organ as a substratum; it is, by definition, diffuse in every reach of society. Nevertheless, it has specific characteristics which make it a distinct reality. It is, in effect, independent of the particular conditions in which individuals are placed; they pass on and it remains. It is the same in the North and in the South, in great cities and in small, in different professions. Moreover, it does not

change with each generation, but, on the contrary, it connects successive generations with one another. It is, thus, an entirely different thing from particular consciences, although it can be realized only through them.[6]

To the nominalistically inclined, such a thing as the "collective conscience" will seem merely the hypostatization of an abstraction. In fairness to Durkheim, what he asserts is that the hypostatization is the other way around: society creates and sustains itself by creating those who are enlisted for life in its service, persons. The individual is not given, but made, and society is his maker. This conception of the human community as a kind of divinity lacks neither philosophical precedents nor prima facie plausibility. Thus we saw in §4.3 that the moral order tends to conceal itself, ruling its creatures rather like a hidden god.

More than an analogy is intended here. Durkheim's last major work, *The Elementary Forms of the Religious Life*, is a study of religion among the Australian Bushmen which endeavors to show how, notwithstanding the diversity of their rites, creeds, and degree of civilization, society is the hidden object of worship of all religions.[7] Radcliffe-Brown writes in the same spirit, "It is perhaps . . . a truism to say that religion is the cement which holds society together."[8] Thus when we survey the institutions, practices, and beliefs of any society—for example, our own—we find that most have readily apparent practical explanations. We eat to avoid starvation and we copulate to propagate the race, and we believe that eating sustains life and copulation makes new lives because these are very practical beliefs to have. Other institutions, practices, and beliefs, however, seem to survive in spite of, or perhaps even because of, their practical uselessness. If we ask a native informant the reason for one of these impracticalities, he may give a practical reason that we think unreasonable ("If we ate these forbidden foods, we would sicken and die"); he may give a supernatural reason; or he may simply say, "But we have always done (believed) this." Durkheim's functionalistic assumption is that the real reason is to be found in the contribution of the institution, practice, or belief to the integrity and solidarity of the society that employs it. This contribution is sometimes called its "latent" (as opposed to "manifest") function.[9] A social system being a system, features of it which appear unreasonable from the standpoint of the individual's physical and psychic needs can sometimes be seen to be essential to the system as a whole, which transcends its individual members. For example, religious sacrifices that are economically unwise, perhaps even calamitous, for the individual and his family may nevertheless be vital to the individual's and the family's sense of their place in the total moral order, in other words, to society's sense of its own selfsameness in spite of the dispersion of its members in time, space, and interest.

Like religious theories of Providence, functionalism's principle that society is reasonably organized seems to invite excess. To say of whatever appears to need explaining that "Society did it" is as tautological as saying "God did it." There seems no reason, however, for supposing functionalism more prone to this form of pathological excess than any other explanatory principle. Earlier in this section, we considered explaining love first as a psychological need, then as a set of moral rules. The principles involved can also be stretched into tautologies, the first by postulating a need for every action, the second by providing a justification for whatever we do.

Functionalism has been accused of a conservative bias. To say that the social order perpetuates itself by creating persons seems to deny the creature both the right and even the ability to criticize his creator. Defenders of the method reply that functionalism is not a first-order justification of the status quo nor of anything else, but a second-order definition of what counts as explaining a social phenomenon.[10] A principle of explanation, after all, is a way of looking at experience. It determines what one will be able to see. We shall examine this controversy in some detail in §11 below.

A preliminary remark may nevertheless be helpful here. The accusation of conservatism depends on interpreting functionalism after the analogy of a religious apologia or a governmental white paper. For a counteranalogy, we may recall the intimate interdependency of society and language. Thus English, like any other natural language, is a world unto itself. Whatever can be said in any language can be said in English. The deep structure of the English sentence is what makes possible this linguistic homeostasis. A theoretical grammar should explain how it does so. Although such an explanation would also be a justification of the deep structure, the sentence is so close to us that we can no more change it than we can step outside the world. It determines our ability to say anything at all, whether radical or conservative. In so far as a social system may be compared to a language, it should have this same foundational or englobing quality.

Functionalism appears to entail a large and disputable ontological claim, a claim peculiarly suspect to the philosophical skeptic, who demands that the existence of entities be demonstrated. Is there really such a *thing* as "society," the enormous, pervasive, self-creating and self-sustaining moral agency of the functionalists? If indeed, as we noted in §4.2, the skeptical tradition requires us to doubt the real existence of such entities as the moral self and the feeling of love, then we are obliged to doubt even more strenuously the existence of the agency said to be responsible for those doubtful entities, an invisible agency whose actions are claimed to be limitlessly profound, but whose spatiotemporal limits are in fact rather ill-defined.

It can be argued, however, that we would do well to look with some skepticism upon this skeptical tradition itself. The tradition takes the reality of philosophical doubt for granted. Its originator, Descartes, simply assumes he can doubt every idea in his mind. He never doubts his own ability to take this initiative. The objects he doubts may not really exist, but his doubting of them must. Philosophical doubt puts its object at risk, but not its subject, not the doubting itself nor the doubter.

One may urge to the contrary, however, that doubting is an action. An action has a definition. What it is can be said of it. And an action, even an intellectual action, has effects or consequences. Whoever takes an action risks its consequences. With a proper skepticism, we should look upon the definition of an action and the risks it entails as coimplicative. What an action really is, surely, is determined by the risks the taker really runs, and conversely. Traditional philosophical doubt is theoretical doubt, doubt that does not run the risks of everyday life but rather the risks of the seminar room. For example, Hume writes:

> My practice, you say, refutes my doubts. But you mistake the purport of my question. As an agent, I am quite satisfied in the point [viz., that the future can be inferred from the past]; but as a philosopher, who has some share of curiosity, I will not say skepticism, I want to learn the foundation of this inference.[11]

But if practice and the practical risks of everyday life are framed out of the apolitical skeptical debates of the seminar room, this means that the society which tolerates and supports philosophical theorizing is framed out also. If one assumes that the skeptical debate can be well-defined and internally consistent independently of society, that very assumption implies that society is well-defined and internally consistent independently of philosophical theorizing. But that is the functionalist's assumption. In short, the traditional skeptic's insulating of philosophy from social life conceals a philosophical positing of the insulation of social life from philosophy. In Part III, we shall question the ontological assumptions underlying functionalism, employing a method different from that of the traditional philosophical skeptic. We shall consider skepticism again in §16.

Durkheim writes:

> A society can neither create itself nor recreate itself without at the same time creating an ideal. This creation is not a sort of work of supererogation for it, by which it would complete itself, being already formed; it is the act by which it is periodically made and remade. Therefore when some oppose the ideal society to the real society, like two antagonists which would lead us in opposite directions, they materialize and oppose abstractions. The ideal society is not outside of the real society; it is a part of it. Far from being divided between them as between two poles which mutually repel each other, we cannot hold to one without holding to the other. For a society is not made up merely of

46

the mass of individuals who compose it, the ground which they occupy, the things which they use and the movements which they perform, but above all is the idea which it forms of itself.[12]

Durkheim's thesis is Greek: a society is an ideal enacting itself in time. This functionalism is not an omnicompetent explanatory principle. No principle is omnicompetent. As students of questions and explanations, we shall find what functionalism cannot explain as illuminating as what it can.

§6 Love as a Public Instrument

We pursued romantic love from feeling to policy to contract to system of moral rules. Each succeeding step produced its increment of enlightenment, but we were still unable to conceive this as a single series based on a clear principle. Therefore in §5 we reconsidered what should count as explaining love. We concluded that such an explanation would be functionalistic.

In this and the following sections of Part II, we want to examine and assess the functionalistic explanation of love. To do so, we must give the explanation first. Giving it is a problem in sociology. We are interested in this problem for its own sake, but we are even more interested in it as an example of one method of explaining love, for it is in that capacity that it advances our philosophical argument. We shall try to construct a plausible sketch of a functionalistic theory. Filling in the details of it must be left to the sociologists, who specialize in these matters, just as the philosopher specializes in theories and questions.

In §2, we noted that sometimes what we need to know in order to explain a concept is what it does, or what its function is. By "function" in that section, we meant what the concept enables the individual to do, that is, what he can do having the concept that he could not do lacking it. While this—Wittgenstein's "tool" analogy—is a useful guide for explaining many concepts, we suggested in §5 that love is much more like a public instrument which society uses to accomplish its collective purposes than like a tool, a private instrument for the accomplishment of individual purposes. Public instruments are called "institutions." The explanation of a concept as an institution will show how society uses the concept to maintain itself through time, through changing physical circumstances, psychic distractions, and the passing of the generations. To show how will mean to show how this institution supports and is supported by society's other institutions.

What, then, is the social function of romantic love? One scarcely knows where to begin with such a large and diffuse question. Perhaps we may find a clue in the concept of the moral and legal orders and their relation developed in §4.3. There we said that the rules defining an official, formal institution will be enforced by law. Where an institution is ambiguous, where there is a question about what its rules really are, this activity of enforcement provides the surest possible test: the rules really prevailing will be those whose violators really do risk punishment. Informal institutions, extending the concept of an institution, are sanctioned by informal social controls such as praise and blame. Here too an institution is defined by its rules, and which rules really prevail is determined by which rules are enforced. Institutions direct traffic among people. The banking system, for a formal example, gives investors and borrowers means for profitable financial cooperation. Its rules are published and legally enforced. This activity of enforcement defines the concept of banking. If one were to ask, "What is banking, really?" there is certainly room for abstract economic speculation about this large question, but in a blunt, obvious sense the question is continually being settled by the statutes and the courts. The economist is free to entertain an original theory of the nature of banking, but courts and legislatures determine what he may act upon. In this sense, the concept of banking is enforced.

When we turn to such an informal institution as romantic love, when we ask, "What is love, really?", we are inclined to suppose the question highly speculative. Love is part of the moral order, and we have seen that the moral order tends to hide itself, leaving us with an apparent freedom to indulge our individual fancies about questions that are in fact collectively settled. Here the implication is plain that we interpret "What is love?" differently from "What is banking?" because the activity of enforcement that defines love is an activity we are supposed to disattend. Accordingly, the functionalistic method suggests that what we should look for in order to define love is this activity of collective enforcement.

John and Marsha exchange vows of love. Not a quarter of an hour later, Marsha discovers John embracing Rosie. John may not excuse himself on the ground that he has his own individual definition of love. Perhaps he has. Who cares? Marsha is not even entitled to accept it as an excuse for his infidelity. What John has violated is not a statute, but is no less plain and definite. The penalties he risks are plain and definite also: some small—or perhaps some large—loss of reputation, and the forfeiture of Marsha's regard. He can, of course, shrug his shoulders and go on to further conquests. No officer will collar him, no magistrate denounce him. The moral order works in more subtle and slipshod ways. The informal social controls that define the concept of love seem dismayingly looser and less reliable than statutes. We noted in §4.3 that the moral order gives rise to the legal order. Where we think informal social controls inadequate, there we pass a law. In this way, moral institutions such as love come to be supported by legal institutions such as marriage, institutions whose meanings are defined by law.

We also noted in §4.3 that the relations between the moral life of the community and its legal armature are complex. Laws do many things besides buttressing points of strain in the moral order. For example, they define weights and measures, establish public holidays, and confer official titles on office holders. If we proceed with caution, however, we may be able to work our way back from what is legally enforced to the informal moral institution which is supported by that activity of enforcement, thus using the legal order as a partial clue to the hidden moral order. The law regulates, but, as the Greeks thought, it also educates. It sets limits to moral activity, but also—and surely more fundamentally—it posts guidelines for moral activity.

In modern Western societies, romantic love is supposed to lead to monogamous marriage. Such a pronouncement seems blunt, but then the law is a blunt moral instrument. The guidelines it posts apply to sophisticated and unsophisticated, hip and square alike, who interpret its simple prescriptions in differently devious ways. Here the prescription is simple enough: when in love, get married. Clearly what love is supposed to lead to furnishes one clue to what love is. Two persons of opposite sex live together, share property, have sexual intercourse, bear and raise children, provide one another approval and emotional support, cherish one another's family ties, and are in manifold ways loyal to one another, all under the sanction of the law. There in outline is the idea and ideal of monogamous marriage. Many of these prescriptions are straightforwardly enforced, marriages being dissolvable on grounds of desertion, refusal to consummate, emotional incompatibility, and so on. If one is asked why one abides by these prescriptions, however—why one lives with and has sexual intercourse with one's spouse, and so on—then in our society, the prescribed answer is not "Because it is my duty" or "Because the law would get me if I didn't," but "Because I love him (her)." But these prescriptions defined monogamous marriage long before romantic love was prescribed as the ground for abiding by them. Nothing in the concept of marriage itself—even in the concept of marriage as a sacrament—necessitates our contemporary use of romantic love as the underlying bonding agent.

We have, then, two questions. Just how does romantic love serve us as the underlying bonding agent in marriages? And why do we collectively employ—indeed, enforce—this bonding agent instead of the historically prominent alternatives, family duty and economic self-interest? These two questions are the first and second stages in a functionalistic answer to "What is love?"

§7 Love as a Bonding Agent: Coded Discourse

Epistemologists are oppressively well-acquainted with the ambiguity of the expression "the reason why X acted as it did." In one sense, a reason is what would explain X's behavior to an expert in explanations of the relevant kind. Thus for the natural scientist, a predictively confirmed general principle coupled with particular boundary conditions implies X's behavior, and there we have the cause of it or the reason for it. Alongside these natural scientist's reasons there are also layman's reasons, which in our society tend to be merely simplified versions of the scientist's reasons. In the social sciences, where what are to be explained are human actions, this neat scheme is complicated by two other kinds of reason. There is what the subject, X himself, thought was the reason why he acted as he did, how he would explain his action to himself. And there is what should have been the reason why he acted as he did, the reason that would justify such an action. Further layers could be interpolated, but these four will do for our purposes.

Since we are concerned with human actions, I shall call the first reason why X acted as he did "the psychological reason," the second "the lay-psychological reason," the third "the subject's ostensible reason" (or "ostensible motive"), and the fourth "the subject's obli gatory reason" (or "obligatory motive"), implying nothing whatever by these expressions and carefully avoiding the expression "actual reason." What complicates the social sciences is the fact that obligatory motives influence ostensible motives, which in turn color lay-psychological reasons. The influence of these complications upon psychological reasons is, of course, a matter of controversy.

Monogamous marriage is an antique institution. If we assume for purposes of argument—it is an exaggeration, but not a wildly unreasonable one—that men and women have always recognized essentially the same prescriptions, always done more or less the same things—lived together, shared property, had sexual intercourse, and so on—in monogamous marriages, then it follows that their actual reasons (whatever in the world those may have been) for behaving in these ways probably have not changed much either. As a matter of historical record, however, their obligatory and ostensible motives have changed radically, and lay-psychological reasons have changed with them.[13] Suppose we define a "social reason" as an obligatory reason in its capacity of dictating or influencing ostensible and lay-psychological reasons. Then by the "underlying bonding agent" for marriages, I mean simply the social reason for them. The clue we are now considering to a functionalistic explanation of romantic love is, then, that in our society romantic love is the social reason for marriage, and we want to understand how and why it so functions.

The social reason for an action functions both as its explanation and its justification. Romantic love is the social reason for marriage by functioning in this dual capacity. Thus if in ordinary circumstances one is asked, "Do you love your wife?" the only proper answer is "Of course," for that is the approved social reason for remaining married to her, at once what is thought to propel one to the action and what makes it right. When Marsha is asked why she wants to marry John, she will invoke love as the reason. The rhetoric or form of discourse she will employ is highly conventionalized. We may speak of a "code," exploiting two of the main meanings of that word: a form of concealed communication, and a system of rules of conduct.

We ask, "Why do you want to marry John?" Consider the following series of answers:

(i) "From the very beginning of time, fate had decreed that he was to be my destiny." (Cosmic necessity.)

(ii) "I knew from the moment I saw him that he was the only one for me." (Predestination, agent unspecified.)

(iii) "I fell madly in love with him the moment I met him." (Irresistible compulsion.)

(iv) "I realized that I had grown to love him and simply had to marry him." (A developed state of extreme need approximating to compulsion.)

(v) "He reminded me so much of my (father/brother/you-name-it) that I couldn't help falling in love with him." (Compulsion as a result of early psychic imprinting.)

(vi) "Oh, I was on the rebound from that awful affair with Sidney, and I guess I was ready to fall in love with the first guy I met." (State of extreme need, approximating to compulsion, in consequence of psychic trauma.)

(I have put in parentheses after each answer what Marsha claims is the causative factor.)

This series progresses from the adolescent's metaphysics of (i) and (ii) to the apparent insight and honesty of (v) and (vi). But if one stops to reflect, it becomes obvious that (vi) is no less literally nonsensical than (i). Thus in (vi), the image of bottled-up feelings—they would have been poured out upon the faithless Sidney—awaiting uncorking by the first passerby, is silly. The coded phrase "I was ready to fall in love with" is synonymous with "I just couldn't resist," and that too is literally nonsense. In clear (that is, decoding), Marsha seems to mean that her unhappy affair with Sidney so shook her confidence in her desirability as a marital partner that she was more than usually anxious to accept an offer, and the best then available was John's.

Here our argument will at first seem especially shaky, for we shall have to rely on words no one ever actually says and on beliefs no one ever quite believes—on greeting-card sentiments, in fact. Rhetoric is a process. Forms of expression and turns of phrase come and go, arising as fashionable glosses on their predecessors and disappearing before livelier newcomers. "Do you understand?" becomes "Do you catch on?", then "Do you get me?", and then "You dig?" Like pop psych, the rhetoric of romance also changes with a journalistic rapidity—far too fast to be caught by a book. On the other hand, romances aim at the relatively permanent merger of the relatively permanent interests of their parties, at the formation of those little deposits of relative immortality, families. What the shifting rhetoric invokes, therefore, are stable beliefs about the self and its fate, beliefs that have not changed in some hundreds of years. These beliefs resemble religious beliefs in that their importance lies not in their truth or falsity, but in what we do with them, in the practical function of the rhetoric based upon them.

"The American credo of romanticism," according to Hunt, consists of at least four beliefs. There is the belief in "one person" or "the only one in the world," the belief that for each individual there is a single predestined romantical partner. Second, one should "fall in love": in the presence of that predestined partner, one is unexpectedly overcome by feelings too powerful to be resisted. Third, "love is blind," for those smitten by it are oblivious to their partners' failings, even when those failings are obvious to everyone else. Finally, "love conquers all": inspired by their feelings, lovers can overcome almost any social or physical obstacle.[14] Soberly set down, these beliefs do not invite the assent of the serious-minded. Since what we do with them is serious enough, the only conclusion possible is that they are the foundation of a coded rhetoric, an extravagant, disguised way of talking.

We decode automatically, for we have been trained not to notice that this rhetoric is literally nonsensical. We have always known that these cosmic necessities and irresistible amorous compulsions are romantic fictions, but because we are supposed to decode automatically, we ignore or disattend this knowledge. Indeed—to say the same—we tend to feel threatened when the magic is exposed, when this knowledge of ours is brought to our attention, for coding is obligatory and enforced.

Code decodes into clear. To say that the social reasons for romantical decisions are expressed in code implies that the same messages could be expressed in another form, a form that sender and receiver alike would acknowledge to be literally true by comparison. One possible approach here is to recall the overworked epigram that the only mystery is that there simply is no mystery. The grounds on which persons choose marital partners are at least as familiar and unmysterious as the grounds on which they make their other major decisions. Those other decisions—choice of a career, political party, place of residence—are virtually always a predictable function of the individual's background and prospects. There is no reason for supposing persons less transparent to one another in their romantical dealings. Indeed, the intense, gossipy interest we take in unexpected decisions demonstrates that the expected usually happens. Looked at in this way, coding really conceals nothing, and since persons' romantical dealings are with one another, this transparency is obviously functional for society as a whole. Further, it makes no sense to suppose that in choosing marital partners on such grounds as proximity, familiarity, physical attractiveness, social prestige, economic advantage, and the like, persons are doing anything except what they ought to do. Our social or moral controls seem to work about as effectively in this department of life as in any other, which entitles us to conclude that persons probably behave themselves reasonably well here. The clear transcription of "Because I love her" and similar statements will differ from individual to individual and from situation to situation, therefore, but not in ways we do not readily understand and cannot readily express in homely, everyday terms. Indeed, considering how little the institution of marriage has changed across the centuries, one may suggest that the immediate and direct effect of coding must not be on what persons do, but on how they tell one another about what they do, therefore also on how they think about themselves as persons who do such things.

Language is presumptively taken to refer to things that exist. If in the ordinary course of conversation I say, "My uncle fractured his skull while mooring his yacht," I shall be taken to have asserted the existence of an uncle, a skull, and a yacht. Many forms of discourse refract or altogether bracket out these ontological commitments, however. Fictional narration is an example: nouns in the frame[15] created by "Once upon a time . . ." do not refer. Metaphor is another: "the fire of his wrath" does not refer to a real fire, though it may refer indirectly to real properties of a real wrath. Coded discourse is a third example. We have seen that there are no good reasons for supposing that nouns in coded discourse correspond one-for-one with referential nouns in clear, and very good reasons for supposing that they do not.

At this point in Part II, accordingly, we have a partial and still abstract functionalistic answer to the question, "What is love?" Love is a noun in romantically coded discourse, a noun referring to forces and feelings alleged to cause and justify certain decisions, of which the decision to marry is the most important. This answer is ontologically biased: nouns in coded discourse refer to real things very indirectly, if they refer to them at all. In clear and in fact, then, there is no such thing as romantic love. This conclusion is morally neutral. It certainly does not imply that our rules for con-

ducting affairs of the heart are somehow wrong. Indeed, we arrived at it by
taking as prescribed that same coded discourse.

In §4.1, we introduced the distinction of primary from secondary relationships, the primary being those that define the individual's selfhood, the
secondary those in which he seeks his advantage. We may recall our functionalistic hypothesis: a society is a moral order, an ideal realizing itself in
the form of individuals. Those individuals must also cope with the physical necessities of life on earth. They are caught, therefore, between the moral order that makes itself concrete through their actions and the demands of
their bodies. Said differently, the moral order exists by at once dispersing
itself in the form of separate individuals and uniting itself through those
individuals' recognition that it is more valuable than they are. By prescribing how the individual shall make the primary-secondary distinction, society tells him how to manage his dual allegiance to itself and to himself—in
other words, how to distinguish what he is from what he consumes. A particular society will do this in a particular way. We can understand, thus,
how desperate times force women to sell their sexual favors, reclassifying as
secondary some aspects of themselves that in more settled times they would
have guarded as primary.

In §4.2, we introduced the distinction between messages intended to establish the moral identity or selfhood of the sender and messages issuing
from him in that identity. We argued on logical grounds that messages of
the first kind must be communicated tacitly. We argued also that, in order
to minimize the risks to the negotiators, negotiation of primary relationships must be fundamentally tacit. In our society, marital relationships are
primary, and therefore the function of coded discourse must be to provide a
channel for negotiating them. What is "tacit" in this channel is the clear
meaning of messages sent on it.

Our code, our romantical rhetoric, is not the only possible intermediary
between marital negotiators. Instead of talking to one another in code, the
parties could employ others as agents or resort to some form of purchase—
both historically prominent alternatives. We should next ask, then, why we
in modern Western societies conduct these affairs in code, and why in just
this particular code, with its long history and its elaborate conventions.

§8 Some Principles of Functionalistic Explanation

Our functionalistic hypothesis is that society is a moral order, an ideal
realizing itself in the form of individuals organized by institutions. A functionalistic explanation of one of those institutions will show how it sup-

ports and is supported by the others, thus maintaining the social system as a whole. We said that romantic love is a primary relationship, a relationship defined by moral rules. We found a clue to the discovery and explanation of those rules in the activity of enforcing them, for while the social controls that enforce this informal, moral institution tend to be hidden, they give rise to the overt, formal, legally enforced institution of marriage. The hidden activity of enforcement may be inferred, therefore, from the unhidden legal institution. Romantic love is supposed to be the bonding agent in or social reason for marriage. This has two meanings: First, lovers ought to do of their own free will what the marriage laws require (and more, of course); second, in conducting such a primary relationship, persons require one another to communicate in a coded rhetoric whose most prominent feature is love, depicted as a potent metaphysical and psychological agent. The second of these senses of "love" is said to be related to the first as cause to effect, hence by metonymy we use the same word to designate the coded noun and the primary relationship.

In §7, I suggested that we might assume for purposes of argument that men and women have always acted more or less the same ways in monogamous marriages, even though the social reasons they have used to explain and justify their actions have changed considerably across the centuries. This obviously exaggerated assumption has the merit of enabling us more clearly to distinguish love as a primary relationship from love as a coded noun. One can argue that the moral decencies of heterosexual domesticity are far older than romantic love. The argument may be questionable, but not the distinction. How we think we should behave is one thing, the rhetoric in which we articulate our thoughts is another.

We asked at the end of §7 why we conduct our romantical affairs in code, and in this particular code. Because of the metonymous ambiguity of "love," these questions as they stand are also ambiguous. Prima facie there seems no reason why what counts as a functionalistic explanation of a primary relationship should be the same as what counts as a functionalistic explanation of the rhetorical code in which that relationship is negotiated. Before undertaking either explanation, therefore, we should be clearer about what sort of thing we are looking for, about what in each case should count as an explanation. Since the relationship is the final cause of the code, we should examine the relationship first.

A moral order, being an order, imposes upon itself "system demands" for consistency and completeness. Primary relationships determine obligations, therefore a moral order will be incomplete without principles for the preferential ranking of relationships. Thus our own society consecrates the ideal of "companionable marriage," marriage in which husband and wife regard the bond between them as the most intimate of their primary rela-

tions, so that in general their obligations to one another will take prece-
dence over their obligations to any third party. (The major exception is the
mother's obligation to her dependent children.) We look upon companionable marriage as the richest and most rewarding of our social relationships, the fitting goal of a lifetime's efforts at sociability. Scanzoni divides
this ideal into three "core elements": each spouse provides the other with
someone to do things with, someone to love, and someone to talk to.[16] In
each of these capacities, husband and wife will find themselves more firmly
bound to one another than to any third party, spending more time in one
another's company, having a greater physical and emotional involvement
with one another, and possessing more information about one another
than about any third person. Here, evidently, is the summit of our hierarchy of primary relationships.

We may note in passing that this ideal is by no means shared by all cul-
tures. Blood, for example, writes that "husband-wife companionship is not
considered important in Japan,"[17] and Vogel, in a study of middle-class
families in a Tokyo suburb, found that "for informal social life, a husband
does not meet with his wife's friends, the wife does not associate with her
husband's friends, and they rarely go out together as a couple."[18] Examples
from other societies and from our own past are easily found, for companionable marriage with its plain implication of female equality consorts
ill with the concept of woman as chattel or with the practice of multiple
childbirths. If the husband's most intimate bond is to his wife, then his
obligations to patron, parents, and male companions will be subordinate.
By definition, preference is a scarce good: one hierarchical arrangement of
primary relationships excludes another.

A functionalistic explanation of a primary relationship will show that
relationship's place in a system of such relationships, the entire hierarchy
being in an obvious way the final cause of each of its members. Explanation
at this level is not very informative, however. When we say we place companionable marriage at the summit of our hierarchy of primary relationships, this ranking in turn raises the question, "But why do we do that?"—
which asks what is the explanation for the hierarchy's being ordered as it is
instead of in some other way.

What counts as an explanation of a society's entire hierarchy of primary
relationships? The very size of a question that asks for the function of an
"institution" in this grand, overarching sense suggests that its answer is
probably implicitly contained in the question itself. In §4.1, primary relationships were said to be moral as opposed to economic, to involve the exchange of goods essentially identical to the exchangers themselves rather
than duplicatable goods such as money, thus to define the persons who
have advantages or disadvantages in contrast to the ways in which they are
advantaged or disadvantaged over one another.

The distinction is equivalent to the Kantian distinction of dignity from price. It seems to be implied in the concept of moral interaction itself. Thus when billiard balls collide in the prototypically causal interaction, the laws governing the collision are obviously not internal to the balls themselves. On the other hand, pedestrians colliding at a corner will say "Excuse me!" or "Why don't you watch where you're going?" and the like. Each passes judgment on his own conduct and the conduct of others, for the rules of these moral interactions are present in the interactants themselves. A moral interactant therefore functions in two capacities: he acts, and he passes judgment on his own and others' actions. What makes the interaction moral is the interactants' mutual recognition of one another's recognition of common standards or rules of conduct. This enables each of them to be at once actor and judge, player and referee. As is indicated in §4.1, primary relationships (or relationships in so far as they are primary, or the primary aspects of relationships) determine the individual's honor, his capacity as a worthy moral judge, a representative of the moral order; secondary relationships determine his relative success or failure in the competitions which that order regulates. The distinction points not so much to two distinct sets of relationships as to two distinguishable moral capacities, concomitantly to two fundamental modes of interpretation of conduct, modes that are supposed to be kept rigidly separate.

Here we may draw upon the familiar game analogy to suggest that both the rules of play and the actual playing of a game are abstract considered by themselves. They refer to one another, and only together make up the game. Thus the individual in his capacity as moral judge, guardian and representative of the moral order, derives his significance from the interest-determined actions which the order rules and upon which he passes judgment. His primary relationships will oblige him to rise above his interests, but what that means will be determined by what counts as an "interest." This is most conveniently thought an economic question. The very concept of interaction between self-regulating representatives of a moral order implies that the nature of their self-regulating capacities will be determined by the nature of the actions they are supposed to regulate. Hence a functionalistic explanation of a system of moral or primary relations must show how that system subserves an economic system, for either of these dimensions of moral interaction is a mere abstraction in the absence of the other.

I have used "moral" and "economic" here as catch-all terms with the intent of holding off ontological commitment as much and as long as possible. A society is at least a moral order. Historically, this moral authority has usually been thought to rest upon a religious sanction, entailing a commitment to the existence of something beyond simply persons acting in concert, namely, something supernatural. Similarly, the individual's self-regarding interests are at least economic, at least proper objects of "rational self-interest" in the economist's sense. Those interests have often been taken to be ultimately biologically determined and physical, entailing a commitment to some form of naturalism. Our functionalism has the advantage of sidestepping both commitments. We assume only that society is a moral order of individuals. It follows from this assumption alone that it must as it were divide itself against itself into two opposed systems of social controls, the one directing individuals how to conduct themselves as representatives of the whole, the other telling them how to conduct themselves as self-seeking individuals. Although both systems are often said to depend upon such external agencies as God and nature, their systematic interplay can be studied quite independently of any ontological underpinning.

This ontological caution has an important consequence, however. If indeed the very concept of a moral order implies that a given society's system of primary relationships and its economic system must be functional coimplicates, then this functional coimplication determines what must be the latent or actual function of primary relationships, namely, their economic utility. Accordingly, whatever in that society may be said to be the reasons for those relationships must be discounted in advance as mere rhetoric. In other words, the functionalistic method of explanation we have chosen (for the purpose, be it noted, of evaluating its explanatory powers) dictates that what may count as the explanation of a primary relationship must ultimately turn out to be its economic function. As we shall see, this economic function may *not* be what is called its "manifest function," that is, what the natives say is the reason for it. Hence it follows from the method itself that what in a given society is the official "thing to say" about primary relationships must be mere rhetoric, a way of saying one thing while really (if no doubt unwittingly) meaning another, the point being that reasons which are not real reasons have nothing else left to be but rhetorical reasons.

Now by definition, the layman cannot give his economic relationships an economic justification. The primary are just those relationships that are supposed to be valuable in themselves, without regard for their (economic) consequences. (Of course a primary relationship may also be valued for its utility, just as an instrumental relationship may also be affectionate or hostile; but these two modes of interpretation are supposed to be kept separate.) On the other hand, since the explanation of a hierarchy of primary relationships, and therefore the ultimate explanation of any particular member of the hierarchy, must be economic, it follows that the function of the rhetoric of those relationships must be precisely to disguise their economic function. In other words, such an elaborately ceremonious manner of speaking as the coded discourse of §7 must be the means by which the moral order at once promotes the economic survival of its members and at the same time establishes in their minds its absolute opposition to that same economic system.

Just as the primary-secondary distinction is implied in the very concept of moral interaction, so also is the necessity that moral rhetoric should perform this dual function. Primary relationships are those in which the individual establishes his capacity as a moral judge, a trustworthy representative of the moral order, while secondary relationships are those in which he competes for survival and advantage. He is at once player and referee, and others obviously depend upon his ability to keep those capacities separate. He must therefore tacitly seek their recognition by portraying himself as a judge equally trustworthy with respect to their moral worth as with respect to his own. They require him to claim that he holds himself— his selfhood, his pride, his honor—above the struggle for survival. Hence the dual function of the rhetoric of primary relationships, the language of oaths, vows, pledges, and promises: it must be well-adapted for promoting the general (economic) welfare, but also well-adapted for enabling the individual to claim that, as a moral man, he rises superior to considerations of mere welfare.

At the end of §7, we asked why we conduct our romantical affairs in code, and why in this particular code. Before we can give a functionalistic answer to these questions, we have the problem of determining what sort of answer we should look for. That rather awkwardly abstract problem has been the topic of this section. We have seen that a primary relationship such as romantic love is to be explained by how it fits into a system of such relationships, and we have seen that the entire system is to be explained by its economic utility. We have seen also that the rhetoric of a primary relationship is to be explained by how it at once promotes the adaptation of the moral order to the economic system and at the same time enables individuals (and, through them, the order itself) to claim that they rise superior to economic considerations. Since the problem of this section is methodological, not factual, we have attempted to give it an a priori solution, deriving that solution from the a priori concept of moral interaction. The next section will consider the application of these principles of functionalistic explanation to contemporary romantic love and coded discourse.

Perhaps that concrete application will help to reduce the obscurity that inevitably accompanies such an abstract argument. It may also serve to reduce that obscurity if we can see how essentially the same conclusions could have been drawn in a different vocabulary. We argued that the primary-secondary or moral-economic distinction is implicitly contained in the concept of moral interaction essential to the functionalistic method. A society must divide itself into two systems—two worlds, as it were—that at once interpenetrate and hold themselves separate from one another. We called these two systems "moral" and "economic" in the interest of ontological parsimony. Allowing for this interest, our moral-economic distinction is essentially identical to the distinction between the "sacred" and the "profane" around which Durkheim builds his well-known definition of religion. He writes,

> But the real characteristic of religious phenomena is that they always suppose a bipartite division of the whole universe, known and knowable, into two classes which embrace all that exists, but which radically exclude each other. Sacred things are those which the interdictions protect and isolate; profane things, those to which these interdictions are applied and which must remain at a distance from the first. Religious beliefs are the representations which express the nature of sacred things and the relations which they sustain, either with each other or with profane things. Finally, rites are rules of conduct which prescribe how a man should comport himself in the presence of these sacred objects. When a certain number of sacred things sustain relations of co-ordination or subordination with each other in such a way as to form a system having a certain unity, but which is not comprised within any other system of the same sort, the totality of these beliefs and their corresponding rites constitutes a religion.[19]

Durkheim's distinction is functionalistic, for, so he asserts, the source of sacredness and ultimate object of worship is society itself. The function of religion for Durkheim is to effect the basic mobilization and organization of actions, beliefs, and sentiments that underlie all society's institutions. It follows, first, that social phenomena not usually labeled "religious" may have a latent religious function, and, second, that none of the many competing sects and creeds of our own pluralistic, secular society can perform this fundamental integrating function. We shall return to this topic in Part III.

Allowing for the connotations of a different vocabulary, Durkheim's sacred-profane distinction can be thought to be already implicit in our primary-secondary distinction. Thus the latter has its ontological ground in the distinction between persons and other things (I shall say simply "things"). Persons are valuable in themselves and persons alone can recognize values. Accordingly, in the order of knowing at least, all other values depend upon the value persons attribute to one another. Persons alone have selves, can converse, deliver insults or compliments, be loving rather than merely lovable. Things are incapable of these accomplishments. Therefore persons are appropriate objects for primary relationships, whereas things are not. Things—animals, for example—may have rights, but only persons can be spokesmen for those rights. By definition, persons and things exhaust the universe.

In "The Nature of Deference and Demeanor," Goffman presents a modern version of Durkheim's functionalistic conception of religion. He undertakes "to explore some of the senses in which the person in our urban secular world is allotted a kind of sacredness that is displayed and confirmed by symbolic acts," acts Goffman summarizes under the headings "deference" and "demeanor." He distinguishes "substantive" from "ceremonial" rules of conduct in this way:

> A substantive rule is one which guides conduct in matters felt to have significance in their own right, apart from what the infraction or maintenance of the rule expresses about the selves of the persons involved.[20]

> A ceremonial rule is one which guides conduct in matters felt to have a secondary or even no significance in their own right, having their primary importance—officially, anyway—as a conventionalized means of communication by which the individual expresses his character or conveys his appreciation of the other participants in the situation.[21]

The individual's selfhood, his pride or self-esteem, can be viewed as a psychological fact, a subjective occurrence that some experiences will tend to enlarge, others to diminish. The structure of this subjective occurrence, however, is determined by the means for expressing it, the code or language that enables individuals to make and accredit claims of worthiness or unworthiness. This code or language is etiquette. Etiquette is the means by which society gives selfhood as a social fact a symbolic independence from selfhood as a psychic occurrence, so that, for example, others are obliged to praise the author of some small accomplishment, no matter how little they may think of it or him, and he is obliged to say, "Oh, it was nothing much," no matter how vain he may feel. Thus positive courtesy images enable individuals to elevate one another's selfhood above the vicissitudes of interaction:

> While it may be true that the individual has a unique self all his own, evidence of this possession is thoroughly a product of joint ceremonial labor, the part expressed through the individual's demeanor being no more significant than the part conveyed by others through their deferential behavior toward him.[22]

The individual demands humane, courteous treatment on grounds of his humanity, and the little ceremonies of etiquette allow others to worship him, granting him his selfhood, his absolute difference from what can be bought and sold, consumed or discarded. Since, as Goffman puts it, "every religious ceremony creates the possibility of a black mass,"[23] negative courtesies—insults, teasings, profanations—also allow others ceremonially to degrade him even while leaving his substantive fortunes intact.

Although the ceremonial and substantive orders entirely interpenetrate one another, they derive their significance from their expressed opposition. They form two worlds, two all-embracing systems of interpretation of conduct, each of which dismisses the other as merely adjectival. Thus although substantive matters are "felt to have significance in their own right" and the ceremonies of etiquette are not, nevertheless the selfhood that these ceremonies make possible is supposed to be valued for its own sake, regardless of its substantive consequences. Because each of these systems maintains its own integrity by dismissing the other, when we look for the contribution of either to the whole this contribution is bound to consist in what it does for the other, there being no third thing with respect to which it might have a function. Thus Goffman writes,

> The rules of conduct which bind the actor and the recipient together are the bindings of society. But many of the acts which are guided by these rules occur infrequently or take a long time for their consummation. Opportunities to affirm the moral order and the society could therefore be rare. It is here that ceremonial rules play their social function, for many of the acts which are guided by these rules last but a brief moment, involve no substantive outlay, and can be performed in every social interaction. Whatever the activity and however profanely instrumental, it can afford many opportunities for minor ceremonies as long as other persons are present. Through these observances, guided by ceremonial obligations and expectations, a constant flow of indulgences is spread through society, with others who are present constantly reminding the individual that he must keep himself together as a well-demeaned person and affirm the sacred quality of these others. The gestures which we sometimes call empty are perhaps in fact the fullest things of all.[24]

What they are full of is significance for the substantive social intercourse they make possible, the point once again being that the ceremonial order is bound to have its function there, since nowhere else is left.

§9 Love at Work: The Utility of the Romantical Emotions

"Love" names a certain primary relationship, a relationship given legal recognition and support through the institution of marriage. "Love" also names the mysterious power—as old as time, as wide as the starry sky, as near as one's innermost soul—which is said to cause that relationship, the entity around which romantic rhetoric is constructed. We know that, narrowly viewed, the function of the relationship is to crown our hierarchy of primary relations and the function of the rhetoric is to serve as bonding agent or social reason for the relationship. But these narrow functions are merely syntactically determined. Beyond them, we want to know what is the function of the entire hierarchy, why the crown and summit of it is justified in code, and why in this particular code. From §8, we know that the entire hierarchy will have an economic function, where "economic" is a catch-all term for all those secondary or bargaining considerations that primary relationships are defined as transcending. We know also that the rhetoric will have the dual function of promoting at once the economic utility of the relationship and the consciousness of it as transcendent. In this section, then, we want to apply these general principles for the functionalistic explanation of primary relationships to the particular case of romantic love in contemporary urban technological society, especially in the United States. In short, we want to determine what love does for us.

In §7, when enumerating the various senses in which something may be a reason for a human action, I avoided assigning a meaning to the expression "actual reason." I did so because the romantical code has a ceremonial, expressive function. It may be compared to the ritualized expressions used on cards of sympathy. No one supposes that "our profound sorrow over your loss" refers to any particular physical or psychological entity. This expression is used to make a stock social move. Its very excess, its exaggeration, signalizes its ritual or ceremonial purpose. "Ritual work," Goffman writes, "is a means of retaining a constancy of image in the face of deviations in behavior."[25] The theorist who undertook to infer a psychology of bereavement from the standard ritualized expressions of sympathy would be thought naive. There seems no reason why we should be less guarded with the romantical code.

No doubt ritualized expressions of sympathy conceal more emotion than they convey, but it does not follow that what they conceal must be selfish, wicked, or dishonorable, nor does anyone suppose this. The same goes for the romantical code. We are trained to discount its literal meaning automatically. Its function is ceremonial rather than substantive in that it prescribes psychological and metaphysical motivations for actions taken, and even tacitly known to be taken, on other (that is, substantive) grounds. In other words, persons do not actually marry, stay married, make sacrifices for, or grant liberties to one another out of love. No cosmic forces nor irresistible feelings compel them, but they do those things because they think it advantageous and honorable that they should—nor is there any reason for supposing they judge less shrewdly or behave less decently in this area of life than in any other. Because the romantical code is used to establish primary relationships, and primary relationships involve promises to transcend selfish or economic motivations, we tend to feel threatened when the code's literally exaggerated, even nonsensical character is pointed out. But the fact that the ritual expressions lovers use for claiming unselfishness are exaggerated metaphors implies nothing whatever about the moral quality of their claims.

What are the actual reasons for romantical actions? The actual reason for anything is what will explain that thing to an expert in that sort of explanation. In other words, an explanation of anything is relative to a theory defining what should count as explaining that sort of thing. Since our purpose in this book is to develop just such a theory of romantic love, we are hardly in a position yet to say what are the actual reasons for romantical actions. When we say, then, that the romantical code has a ceremonial, expressive function, no behavioristic nor reductionistic theory of motivation is implied.

When we say the code has an expressive function, we do mean that the directions it gives are concealed within a view of human nature, a lay psychology. The code tells us what we should do, but it tells us this indirectly, by portraying certain desires and emotions as normal, healthy, and natural. Nothing is more natural, we think, than for such a powerful emotion as love to lead to such a consequential act as marriage. But it is because we think the act so consequential that we credit those who wish to undertake it with powerful emotions. "Why do you want to marry John?" "But we're in love!" Now there is a *good* reason. The only possible counterrejoinder is "Well, you're not, really. You only think you are." Here the directive function of the psychology becomes apparent.

Our concept of how human beings are motivated, our lay psychology, enters into the definition of every one of our institutions. Therefore, if we wish to examine it by itself in order to determine how it functions to maintain our social system, inevitably we must employ cross-cultural comparisons. The most revealing of these will be with the past of our own society, since that is what our present arose in opposition to; here the comparison is not an anthropologist's artifact, but an historical experience. The romantical code grew out of the courtly love of medieval France. Courtly love was a countermatrimonial practice, an idealized adultery. The knight—for only a person of aristocratic rank can feel such an emotion—is supposed to be seized by an overwhelming passion for a lady. She should be his social superior, therefore unattainable. Indeed, as a rule both will be married to others, and he may never have actually seen her. Her function is to serve not as a sexual outlet, but as an embodiment of the ideal, a focus for chivalric fervor. By a solemn vow, the knight dedicates his life to his lady's service. He worships her in secret at first. Then he reveals himself, humbly and gradually, and she grants her recognition, her "favor," gradually and grudgingly. Favor may advance to the stage of nude sex play, but not to actual intercourse, which would be vulgar. The relationship, after all, is supposed to be rewarding in itself, or for the spiritual elevation it provides.[26]

A society draws its motivational rhetoric from what is by definition its most privileged stratum. The frog transformed by the maiden's kiss does not turn into a simple peasant. Courtly love arose in opposition to courtly marriage, marriage as practiced by great landholding, aristocratic "lines" or "houses." (A "line" consists of all the descendants of a common ancestor.) It celebrated the knight's devotion to his lady whom he himself selected in contrast to his everyday duties to his wife, the spouse selected for him by the interests of his line. Ariès writes,

> One has the impression that only the line was capable of exciting the forces of feeling and imagination. That is why so many romances of chivalry treat of it . . . . One might say that the concept of the line was the only concept of a family character known to the Middle Ages.[27]

The line possessed its wealth in the form of land, land retained through the process of inheritance. Therefore the line had an obvious interest in suppressing its members' individual marital preferences and an equally obvious interest in a rhetoric praising obedience, faithfulness, and responsibility. The utilitarian relationship of marriage was contracted primarily by lines, only derivatively by husband and wife. The formal, businesslike character of their relationship, its lack of affective spontaneity, was reinforced by the crowding common in medieval households, where many ages and ranks endured one another's immediate presence by means of a fragile network of privileges and obligations. Children, like wives, were of interest not in themselves primarily but rather as solutions to the problem of sustaining and advancing the fortunes of the line. The modern concept of the affectionate nuclear family was quite unknown.[28]

Primary relationships define the individual. They locate him in the human landscape. Therefore a society's conception of them must change very gradually. In examining the slow transition from the medieval conception of marriage and the family to the modern, we should concentrate on the problem of mate selection, for that is where the romantical code has been most influential. In the twelfth-century Courts of Love, it was maintained that love is not possible between husband and wife. By the close of the middle ages, love had become at least a possibility in marriage and a possible reason for marrying.[29] From that time until quite recently—for the theme is barely outworn—the conflict between love and duty has been a literary staple. Love, of course, has conquered completely, so that in a modern industrial society, it would be thought shameful to marry for any other reason.

We may leave the details of this transition to the social historian. Its economic function is apparent enough. The old rhetoric of duty, obedience, and self-denial aimed to stabilize an agrarian subsistence economy where the household was the principal unit at once of production and consumption. The individual inherited his economic function along with his family name; he was born into a work team. The household's short-term welfare depended on adjusting consumption to production, its long-term survival on solving the problem of inheritance. For both purposes, the individual should be trained to keep his place, subordinating his ambitions to the larger needs of his house.

The subsistence economy of the middle ages was organized around a large number of households, each a virtually self-sufficient unit. It was to the advantage of the household itself to be large, thus assuring an unfailing supply of workers and a finer division of labor. A division of labor entails a system of differential rewards, the greatest necessarily going to the principal manager, the head of household, and his chief lieutenant, his wife. Production was the problem, consumption being guaranteed by the exigent conditions of medieval life.

Contrast with this a modern mass-production economy. Here a relatively few large and efficient production units require a supply of workers and a division of labor greater than any single kinship group, however extended, can supply. Consumption is the problem, not production. Production is organized bureaucratically through a rigorous standardization both of production roles and products. Particularistic kinship ties are incompatible with the universalistic criteria of standardization. Therefore the household has become a consumption unit exclusively, its members being independently recruited for the world of work. High consumption is fostered by increasing the number but decreasing the size of these consumption units, for each requires a "standard package"[30] of goods and services to be recognizable to itself as a household, and every head of household requires the standard tokens of office. Production units, thus, tend to grow ever larger and consumption units—households—ever smaller.

We may ask what organization of subjective sentiments, especially as regards the crucial problem of mate selection and household formation, is functional for such an organization of production and consumption. Here the fact of standardization (and mobility, which comes to the same) is essential for productive efficiency. Individuals must be trained to shape themselves to the requirements of large, bureaucratic organizations, organizations employing standardized workers to produce standardized products.

But these in-fact standardized individuals must also be trained not to deny themselves but instead to celebrate their uniqueness, their individuality, their worthiness, by luxuriating in consumption. For this purpose, individuals should be made anxious to form independent households and assume the head-of-household's role, a role now become more reward than task. A producer needs as much as will enable him to fulfil his production role, but nothing is too good for the consumer. Consumption displays that would be distracting and disruptive at the work place may safely be witnessed and applauded in the privacy of the home. The fact of human standardization, then, must be concealed behind the illusion of uniqueness and individuality, the fact being required for the public world of production, the illusion being supplied by the sharply separated private world of consumption, that is, by the family.[31]

Here the utility of the romantical emotions becomes obvious, as obvious as the message on a mass-produced greeting card. Individuals are trained so that the economic system may be efficient in two interdependent and yet apparently incompatible ways. Efficiency of production requires rationalization: a maximum of output is to be accomplished with a minimum of resources, and in the face of constant change. In order to serve the production system, individuals should be machinelike economic men, standardized workers who subordinate such individualistic factors as tradition and sentiment to calculated expediency. They should have strong deferred-gratification patterns, a lively competitive urge, and a Scroogelike selfishness. Efficient consumption requires the opposite motivations. There a maximum of squandering should be accomplished upon a minimum of pretexts. Individuals should want to want, should be encouraged to fantasize unending and ever-increasing gratification. Their strongest drive—for men are social animals—is for one another's approval, so they should aim at an unqualified approval, an unlimited intimacy. They should, then, be efficiently standardized and selfish men at work, but romantic lovers at home, producing in one world, consuming in the other, and keeping the two sharply separated.

The maiden's prince in shining armor appears suddenly, unexpectedly. He is a reward she did not earn, something she can consume without having first had to produce something else of equivalent value, and she is supposed to rejoice in her good fortune, to think how lucky it was they found each other. The whole purpose of this rhetoric is to contrast the world of work's gradual, painstaking accumulations, its haggling and drudgery, with the sudden, unlooked-for, and undeserved rewards of romance. Of course courtship today is in fact as deliberate and laborious a process of negotiation as it was when county families dickered over dowries or great princely houses forged alliances. Perhaps the modern maiden's teeth have

67

been straightened; perhaps she has been sent to college. Her marriage, however, will unite not two producing corporations, but two consuming individuals, and her parents may glow with pride, but not with profit.

One of the major themes of modern history is the growth of individualism, a concept more easily revered than defined. Perhaps one reason we find it so difficult to say what we mean by "individualism" is that the individual as such is only one side of what we revere, the obverse of a coin whose reverse is the family. Ariès writes,

> The whole evolution of our contemporary manners is unintelligible if one neglects this astonishing growth of the family. It is not individualism which has triumphed, but the family.[32]

But this too is a half-truth, for what modern societies hold sacred is neither individual nor family alone, but both in relation. Individualism makes the wheels of production turn so much the faster, hence the marketplace institutionalizes self-aggrandizement and the acquisitive drives. But acquisitions must be consumed and selfhood displayed before an audience—not before one's competitors, surely, but before that special, private, receptive audience that is the family. Within the home, the rugged individualist becomes the warm, indulgent, unrugged lover. Neither role makes sense without the other. The two are overtly held apart and thought opposites, but their underlying function is to complement one another.

Once upon a time, clerics, maiden aunts, hired men, and other varieties of servant were commonplace. Whole categories of persons did not marry, and romance was the privilege of the privileged few. Today, the economy that abounds in good nourishment and medical care, housing, automobiles, attractive clothing, and university educations is spiritually abundant too, and encourages every man to think himself a prince, every woman to think herself a princess, fit partners for a storybook relationship. The middle-class ideal of suburban domesticity dominates the industrialized nations of the world. We have seen how this marriage of love with heavy industry is functional. By regarding romantic love as the most precious of our primary relationships, we encourage the formation of nuclear families, multiplying the number of consuming units, therefore also the number of masters and mistresses, dissolving ties to kin and locality. A society with the largest possible number of chiefs and the fewest possible number of Indians generates the largest possible demand for headdresses and wampum belts and can the more quickly reshuffle its tiny tribes. Love is our greatest good, and yet no bargain. The vague emotional bond that unites husband and wife transcends the well-defined secondary relationships of the marketplace, but it also therefore does not interfere with those relationships. The rhetoric of romance enables us to combine two apparently contradictory moralities, the one enjoining efficiency, the other commanding indulgence, both together keeping consumption abreast of production.

§10 Dysfunctional Doubts

When we first asked "What is love?" we took the question to be a psychological one, a question that asks how to define a certain intimate feeling. Then we looked more closely at this feeling and saw instead a policy whose objective is a contractual relationship. Policies and contracts are actions, and so love now seemed to be more aptly called an action than a feeling, though feelings are of course involved in it. This action in turn derives its meaning from the moral rules governing it. The act of legislating those moral rules is logically prior to and therefore more genuinely an action than the act of following them. The former is the act of society itself, or of all of us collectively; the latter is the act of each of us individually. Romantic love as an institution makes possible individual lovers with their feelings and contracts and their obligatory ways of talking about those feelings and contracts. So we moved from asking "What does love feel like?" to asking "What do lovers promise one another?" and from there to asking "Which institution is love?" Our functionalistic method defines institutions by their functions, and so in the last section we asked "What does love do for society as a whole?"

If we think of the philosopher as a specialist in questions, then he might better be said to have not so much a position as rather a movement from question to question. A form of questioning and its concomitant principle of explanation will have a limited effectiveness. If we push such a form or principle beyond its limits, then we will encounter tautology, edification, dogmatism, partisanship—the pathologies of explanation—and we will sense that the movement of inquiry has stalled. Thus "What does love feel like?" almost wears its futility on its face, even though a vast literature tries to answer this question. After all, love feels like—that is, resembles—a variety of other feelings: friendship, sexual excitation, contentment, homesickness, and so on. Assessing these resemblances is a game without rules, for circumstances can be imagined in which any one of them could be said to be more accurate than the rest. If we nevertheless prefer some over others, it cannot be on the basis of evidence, but only as a disguised directive, a covert edificatory appeal. Strictly speaking, no particular feeling exactly resembles any other; but that is a tautology. Either way, the question leads nowhere. Our explanation of love as a social institution, however, explains both the psychology of it and the rhetoric of it, tells why some feelings are appropriate to it and some are said to be appropriate to it. The sociological explanation contains the psychological and lay-psychological ones.

We may draw the methodological moral that when the movement of inquiry stalls, when we encounter tautology and the like, then we ought to cast about for ways to widen the context of questioning, for clues to a better concept of what should count as an explanation. Those clues are bound to be concealed somewhere in our former way of questioning, for to ask a question means to select, to single out something as worthy of being questioned. What we leave in will be a function of what we leave out, a function thus of what serves as the disattended background against which our question is asked. Thus when we asked "What does love feel like?" we singled out the range of feelings as the locus of possible answers. Feelings are defined by contrast with actions, here in particular with those actions that are promises, contractual proposals. When we examined figure and ground, feelings and contracts together, then we began to see a better way of asking "What is love?", namely by asking "What do lovers promise one another?" Lovers' promises are individual actions that we single out against the background of the collective moral legislation that makes them possible. We saw in §5 that a conventional ethical inquiry into the question "Which contractual relationship is love?" or, more simply, "What do lovers promise one another?" would be incomplete, for it prescribes an answer in terms of individual actions alone. Therefore, again putting foreground and background together, we turned to functionalism and asked "What does love do for society as a whole?"

In the last section, we found that love has an economic function. It serves as the indispensable counterfoil to competition, the latter grounding a morality of productive efficiency, the former a complementary morality of high consumption. We arrived at this conclusion by comparing contemporary industrial society with early medieval Europe, Europe around the time when courtly love was first practiced. We could have reasoned from a comparison with a society unrelated to our own, a primitive society for example. Reasoning from a comparison with our own past has the advantage that we do not need to invent relations between the two societies compared. It has the disadvantage that we are prone to read the present into the past, finding our ancestors sympathetic where we ought to find them merely alien. This tendency leads us into psychological anachronisms.

It is a long way from the castles of medieval France to the back seats of American automobiles or the lyrics of Japanese popular songs, but courtly love is still recognizable in romantic love today, especially in the American romantical credo stated in §7. Because we are trained to think romantic love a natural capacity of the human race rather than a historically contingent expressive mechanism or code, it is a useful corrective to consider what did not come into being in the late eleventh century, for no new psychological entity, no novel form of experience entered the world then. Men and women have always found one another physically attractive, enjoyed one another's companionship, been kind and loyal to one another. That peculiar mixture of lust and longing we call "infatuation" is a definite experience, a particular kind of passive episode. In so far as romantic love is grounded in a particular feeling, infatuation would appear to be the feeling involved. It is, however, if not part of our evolutionary heritage, at least much older than romantic love. Sappho records its symptoms. What came into being in the late eleventh century was a new way of making expressive use of infatuation, a new form of self-dramatization.

Such a conclusion will be offensive to the layman. Infatuation—as the word itself suggests—is a feeling of no particular dignity, and in everyday life, "dramatizing oneself" means faking what ought to be sincere. The layman will object, then, that our conclusion depends on using "feeling" with an obtuse and impertinent precision, while he himself uses the word broadly to cover both brief episodes of passivity and the presumed ground of mature courses of action requiring forethought, self-discipline, and years to execute. I hasten to concede that this objection is valid from the layman's point of view. Our strategy has been to interpret the lay distinction of feeling from action as if it were psychologically precise, with the intention of showing that the psychology involved is a lay psychology whose purpose is to guide action, not to achieve theoretical precision. We have seen that good reasons for romantical decisions are called "feelings." The layman's purpose in so classifying them, however, is to distinguish the "personal" or "private" decisions he makes as a family member from the impersonal decisions he makes as an economic man. The latter are taken to be challengeable on grounds of rationality and efficiency; the former are not. The lay concept of feeling thus serves as a shield or buffer between domestic consumption morality and the economic morality of the market place. The layman uses it to draw a veil over his private affairs, as is his right, a right we shall explore in more detail in Part III.

In §4.3, we said that the moral order tends to hide itself. It socializes persons by shaping their sense of what is fitting, training them to find some actions and situations easeful and natural, others strained and uncomfortable. The most important actions governed by this training are the displays of moral fitness, of correct attitude and belief, that we demand from one another. These displays are addressed to the necessities of practice, not theory. The rhetoric in which they articulate themselves may be theoretically imprecise, but it has a practical purpose. In everyday life, what we say about love and the other social feelings is what convention obliges us to say, and one violates those conventions at one's peril. A theory, however, is objective by definition. Clearly, then, the major part played in obligatory displays of good character by "the right things to say" about the social feelings threatens our ability to be objective about those feelings and hence to theorize about them. Thus the moral order is hidden, and to uncover it, we need a principle of objectivity, some method enabling us consciously and demonstratively to decode these obligatory displays. This method is, of course, functionalism.

We assume that society acts so as to preserve itself. It exists only through the actions of individuals, therefore it will create individuals motivated to serve it. They, however, will often be quite unaware of the collective ends their individual actions serve, for it will often be a condition of collective accomplishment that their attentions be focused upon each other rather than upon society as a whole. Our method directs us to take the point of view of the whole. Exactly how this is possible is not clear, and we shall return to the problem in Part III. But we assume society is justified in requiring us as laymen to profess—sincerely—a number of ostensible beliefs where our actual beliefs (as indicated by our actions) are different. The romantical code is rich in examples. Thus we say and often believe that we cannot control our romantical feelings, although every evidence indicates that we can and do.

And should. A functionalistic explanation establishes the meaning of an institution by showing it well-adapted to the attainment of society as an end, the justification of this end being assumed. We ourselves are the only possible judges of what is well- or ill-adapted. Thus in the present argument, we serve as our own anthropologists. We try to show how the natives' strange mating customs really do contribute to their way of life, where we ourselves are those natives. Both the sense of what is fitting and reasonable which we explain and the sense of what is fitting and reasonable to which we appeal are our own: we merely shift the same reason from one station or perspective to another. This is a significant shift, however, for private moralizing and functionalistic explanation operate on different levels of generality. What seems reasonable to the acting individual need not coincide with what disciplined reflection shows to be reasonable for society as a whole. Thus, pursuing the example of controlling one's romantical feelings, we have argued that individuals ought to think they choose their marital partners on irresistible impulse, for the distinction of economic from domestic morality depends on their thinking so. This official illusion of compulsion ought to conceal careful calculation, however, for otherwise they would choose badly. Such a conclusion may be displeasing to laymen, but this in no way invalidates it, for a theory is addressed to experts and aims not to please but to prove.

In summary, then, our functional theory concludes that romantic love is a code or expressive mechanism, a stylized, ceremonious utilization of the psychology of infatuation. This code is to be explained by the contribution it makes to our affluent way of life. In that way of life, production is motivated by the selfish competitive urge, but love motivates consumption, and as a result the imperative of "more and more" is satisfied in two apparently contradictory but actually complementary ways. We are entitled to draw this conclusion in spite of the layman's distaste for it, for it is a theoretical conclusion reached from the point of view of society as a whole, while the layman's distaste reflects merely the limited perspective of individual action.

We may dismiss, then, sentimental objections to this functionalistic theory of the sentiments. These objections are, in fact, among the items the theory explains. Objections really damaging to the theory accept its explanation of the function of love, but argue further that on this very basis love is dysfunctional or destructive of the social whole. We shall examine four such dysfunctional doubts. I present them briefly and sketchily because they argue negatively, arguing that love is a bonding agent maladapted to our society. This implies that something else—which is never named— would be well-adapted or functional. Because the positive basis of these negative arguments is not specified, they tend to be inconclusive and unsystematic. They might be and indeed have been much elaborated upon. And I present them informally, for that is how they will be familiar, not as conclusions rigorously derived from well-defined premises, but as doubts, diffuse discomforts, vague suspicions that all is not well with romantic love, that the morality which officially obligates us at the same time leads us where we sense we should not go.

Society lives through the activity of socialization. The family is society's primary socializing agency. Our dysfunctional doubts are usually taken to concern the destructive effects of urbanization and industrialization upon the family. They will be familiar in that form. Since the family is the product of the emotional bonds that unite it, however, we may interpret these doubts as if they were doubts about the functional utility of the romantical emotions themselves. Ralph Linton writes,

> The unparalleled expansion of western European and American economy in the past century, with the wealth of individual opportunity which it has produced, has struck at the very roots of consanguine [i.e., extended] family organization. Moreover, the increase in spatial mobility which came with the opening of new areas to settlement and the development of modern methods of transportation made it easy for the ambitious individual to sever his kin ties by the simple process of moving away. At present the consanguine family retains its functions only in long-settled rural districts and in the case of a few capitalist dynasties. In both instances the advantages of membership outweigh the disadvantages. The average city dweller recognizes his extended ties of relationship only in the sending of Christmas cards and in the occasional practice of hospitality to visiting kin.[33]

We are free to love whomever we please and to live with our lovers wherever we please, away from the censorious eyes of parents and in-laws, each nu-

73

clear family by itself on its own plot of ground or shut up in its own apartment. Wittgenstein writes that "The human body is the best picture of the human soul."[34] What we really value, however, is shown by how we choose to live, and how we choose to live is revealed by the structures we build to live in. The soul reveals itself better in the suburbs it constructs than in the body it only appropriates, and in the suburbs, opportunities for dyadic sexual intercourse are built in, while opportunities for frequent social intercourse outside the family circle are not: we value the marital bond, but not batch living. A suburban population in an automotive civilization approaches a certain maximum dispersion. The price, as is well known, is an omnipresent loneliness.

The effect of this dispersion upon the aged will be familiar. Romantic rhetoric is keyed to the drama of courtship. It celebrates youth, good health, and vitality. It places the highest value on sexual attractiveness. This quality is of course not universally possessed, and the aged conspicuously lack it. Americans tend to perceive one another as potential sexual partners and rivals and to value one another commensurately, a tendency unrelentingly reinforced by commercial advertising. Neglect of the aged is a direct consequence. The old man, the old woman cannot play the romantic hero or heroine. Ugliness and infirmity unfit them for the parts. Having no future worth speaking of, they cannot live happily ever after. Possibilities cling like lint to the young and sexy, but the old are a bore.

Love is said to be a feeling. We have undertaken both to question and to interpret this lay-psychological classification. We have seen that love has a basis in feeling, strictly so-called, not merely in the commonplace sense that lovers will tend to feel favorably disposed and sexually attracted to one another, but also in the psychologically more interesting sense that the rhetoric of love, the romantical code, is built around the feeling of infatuation. Love, like infatuation, is supposed to be wild and foolish, for reasons discussed in §9.

Here a third doubt may trouble us. In an obvious sense, no one save the involved individuals themselves knows what actually goes on in the minds of lovers. In a deeper, general sense, however, the best clue to what persons think is how they talk, for thought is limited by the vocabulary available for expressing it. In our society, the key ritual formula "I love you" must be uttered in an extravagant way, for love is said to be an extravagant emotion. Theodorson writes,

> A final essential characteristic of the romantic value complex is a de-emphasis on the fulfilment of specific expectations in the marriage relationship, and in its place an emphasis on generalized feelings of affection and trust which are combined with an idealization of the future marriage partner.[35]

Traditional societies prescribe the duties of husbands and wives in great detail. We rely instead on vague feelings and an inflated rhetoric, neither of which is of much help in trouble. Mutual agreement about how to cope with disputes and calamities becomes so much the more difficult when neither partner can say exactly what are the contents of the agreement being renegotiated. So an ever-accelerating divorce rate demonstrates that romantic love is a weak bonding agent. Linton's bland assertion that "A marriage which does not satisfy the needs of the partners is nonfunctional, and in a modern world there is little reason for insisting on its continuation"[36] is at best the easy half of the hard truth that no one knows quite what to do with those obvious little reasons, the children. Romantic rhetoric invites couples to define their needs by their dreams. The results are at once predictable and deplorable.

A fourth doubt concerns the effect of love on women. The courtly lover idolized his beloved, and the romantical code has prescribed this idolatry every since—it is perhaps the code's most persistent single feature. The idol plays a passive role. It is the object of someone else's thoughts and feelings. Its own thoughts and feelings are less important. This division of rhetorical labor gives rise to an excessively familiar lay psychology according to which men are active, aggressive, and competent, while women are passive, submissive, and weak. Men therefore are naturally qualified for rewarding lives in the world of work, while women are naturally qualified to stay at home and be loved. Women are thus condemned to lives of parasitism and drudgery, and society is robbed of what half its membership might have contributed—a harsh and increasingly popular indictment.

Of course this short list of doubts could be long extended. For example, one might argue, either as an amplification of our last doubt or as an additional doubt, that men in their masculinity have suffered as badly as women in their femininity from the artificial excesses of the romantical code. And of course love can be defended. Thus there is evidence that extended family ties retain their vitality even though the extended family has scattered, so that our first doubt is overstated.[37] Is, then, our institution of romantic love positively or negatively functional, beneficial or harmful to society as a whole? The question seems the inevitable outcome of the argument we have pursued, but it also seems patently unclear. How could it be settled? What would count here as proof? Here our grasp of the method of the argument begins to falter, and we ought to ask how we arrived at such a question and what can be said for and against its legitimacy as a question. We may hope in this way to get some sense of the limitations of the functionalistic method.

What is the net worth of any major social institution? On the one hand, nothing seems less surprising than to find that such a large, vague moral question is difficult, perhaps impossible to settle. Each of us comes to it with his own peculiar insights, interests, and predilections, and since these differ, our answers will differ too. On the other hand, love is not merely another major social institution, but—arguably, at least—that institution to which we find ourselves most intimately close. Usually when we argue as moralists or social critics, we claim an insight into eternal truths or universally valid principles established by reason or revelation or some other transcendent agency. We claim to stand on some moral Archimedean point outside of society. Functionalism may be taken to be simply the methodological assumption that there is no such point. As moralists, accordingly, we are exposed to the sociological objection posed in §5, that only by adopting the objective, value-neutral standpoint of the sociologist can we obtain a clear view of the institution we presume to judge. Before passing judgment on romantic love, we have to identify it, to determine exactly what it is. The difficulty of doing so is notorious. Therefore, in order to disentangle what we really think love is from what genuinely dangerous conventions oblige us to say and think it is, we need a powerful check on our introspection. This check is the "methodological atheism"—to borrow a term from Weber—of the functionalistic method. In order to determine what our institution of romantic love really is, we set aside moralizing; we assume—as a methodological posture—that society is reasonably put together. As moral critics, we may find love unreasonable in this way or that, but there we are *engagé*, in the battle rather than above it, and the sociologist is entitled to dismiss us on the ground that we literally do not know what it is we are criticizing.

We noted in §5 that functionalism has been accused of a conservative bias by such critics as conflict theorists and radical sociologists. The assumption that society is homeostatic clearly invites such an accusation. Robert Merton is generally credited with the introduction of major refinements in functional theory tending to soften the force of this accusation. One may analyze society as a whole or some part of it; there are, therefore, "levels of functional analysis." One social institution may be dysfunctional for another or for society as a whole, so one may speak of the "net balance" of the functions and dysfunctions of an institution either for another or for society as a whole. Actions authorized by an institution may have "unanticipated consequences," that is, the functions of an institution may be "manifest," consciously intended, or "latent," apparent only to the sociological observer. Given these refinements, Merton can then argue that some institutions are, manifestly or latently, dysfunctional for others or even for society as a whole, thus avoiding the seemingly dubious optimism of unrefined functionalism.[38]

Of course we have made crucial use of Merton's distinction of latent from manifest functions in our own functionalistic analysis of romantic love. Moreover, our analysand is society as a whole, not some part of it. Thus we argued in §8 that, by definition, a society's system of primary relationships and its economic system must be functional coimplicates, though the function of the former for the latter must be latent. Combining these two features of our argument, it would appear that in all consistency we can give the concept of a dysfunction at most a provisional use. Thus if the principle that society acts reasonably is the clue to the discovery of latent functions, when we find an apparent dysfunction, all this can possibly prove is that we should look further. This conclusion may be uncomfortable, but it does seem quite unavoidable.

The concept of society as a whole is the fundamental methodological principle of our functional analysis. Society as a whole has a logical and moral status altogether different from the statuses of the institutions, structures, and individuals that make up society. It has a different logical status, for we do not explain it, but we use it to explain them. Therefore it also has a different moral status, for we explain them by assuming that they are defined by the reasonableness it confers on them. Until we have found that reasonableness, we are not entitled to assume that we have found them as they really are, instead of as they merely appear to be from the perspective of the *engagé* layman.

However, if the concept of society as a whole is a quite special concept to the functionalist, romantic love is a quite special institution too. Our sense of reasonableness is the result of our socialization. We may distinguish the "primary socialization" by which the individual becomes simply a member of society, a sane person equipped with a language, intelligible beliefs, and appropriate emotional responses, from "secondary socialization," by which the individual acquires an additional occupational or organizational identity.[39] Primary socialization creates the substance of the self, secondary socialization decorates that substance with accidents. The main agency of primary socialization in our society is the family, which is held together by primary bonds, romantic love being chief among them. Thus the individual is trained first to be a family member, only afterwards to be also a sociologist, socialist, or stockbroker. The family gives him his identity. When it teaches him how to talk, it also teaches him who is talking. Identity in our society will include at least age, sex, social class, and race,[40] all matters where the family gets its word in first—and also last, for it looks on over the individual's shoulder all his life long. Parsons writes,

> The family . . . can be seen to have two primary functions, not one. On the one hand, it is the primary agent of socialization of the child, while on the other it is the primary basis of security for the normal adult.[41]

Given that the family performs this indispensable primary socialization function, our dysfunctional doubts acquire a special bite. In the functional analysis of §9 we took an institution already defined by its function and showed how it performs that indispensable function in a manner advantageous to a mass-production, high-consumption economy. In that sense, therefore, our dysfunctinal doubts are proposed from the functionalistic standpoint itself, rather than from some Archimedean point outside society. The criticism is internal. From birth to death, the family is the individual's fundamental link to society at large, and if the family tends increasingly to abandon the individual in childhood or old age, or to condemn females to domestic servitude, or simply to dissolve under the individual's feet, one can only conclude that there society turns upon itself and destroys itself.

We said that a fact is a fact relatively to that principle of explanation with which one would defend its factuality. The function of a principle of explanation, so conceived, is not to set antecedently given facts in order, but to define what counts as a fact of a certain sort—a fact of physics, sociology, art history, or the like. Therefore a principle of explanation is not exposed to rejection on grounds of factual inaccuracy. Any fundamental principle of explanation is tautological in this sense. Therefore the objection so often urged against functionalism—that it is tautological[42]—is irrelevant. The dysfunctional doubts we have sketched out here make a straightforwardly empirical claim. Our problem accordingly becomes to understand how such a claim and a principle of explanation can be made to meet on the same logical level, or why any such dysfunctional doubts, no matter how internal and no matter how well supported, should not be rejected on the methodological ground that they may—indeed, must—represent merely *engagé* sentimentalism. If we adopt a method, so we may say, then we really do adopt it, not some version of it compromised by concessions to lay belief and lay sentiment.

Our general aim is to give an account of the question "What is love?" We have transformed this into a functionalistic question, and we have given it an appropriately functionalistic answer. Our aim in this section is to determine the limits of this functionalistic explanation of romantic love. Here we may argue, on the one hand, that such apparently dysfunctional phenomena as conflict, change, and alienation are surely not beyond the limits of functional analysis. If they were, functionalism would indeed generate only tautologies. Rather, functional analyses as we actually find them in sociology attempt to explain conflict, change, and alienation as appearances of an underlying stable substance, to show how society manages to maintain itself in spite of them, in fact, by means of them. Thus *Stigma*, Goffman's study of the life situation of individuals with discrediting or discreditable social handicaps, concludes:

> And although it can be argued that the stigma processes seem to have a gen-

eral social function—that of enlisting support for society among those who aren't supported by it—and to that degree presumably are resistant to change, it must be seen that additional functions seem to be involved which vary markedly according to the type of stigma. The stigmatization of those with a bad moral record clearly can function as a means of formal social control; the stigmatization of those in certain racial, religious, and ethnic groups has apparently functioned as a means of removing these minorities from various avenues of competition; and the devaluation of those with bodily disfigurements can perhaps be interpreted as contributing to a needed narrowing of courtship decisions.[43]

Herbert Gans' article, "The Positive Functions of Poverty," conforms to the same logical model.[44]

On the other hand, however persuasive such examples as these may be, either the first and defining principle of functional analysis—that collective activity which maintains its own selfsameness, society—has a content, or it does not. If it does not, if "society" names merely a formal principle of method, then functionalism becomes an abstract injunction to be objective about social institutions, and we may rightly ask, "But what are they, and how should one be objective about them?" And these questions will be unanswerable. If, however, the principle does have a content, if society is assumed to be a definite end attainable by definite means, then that methodological assumption itself limits the method, for it is the limit that the method proposes for itself. From this assumption, however, three puzzling consequences follow. First, it will then be possible to entertain, as we have, dysfunctional doubts about the factual accuracy of this assumption, for so grand and absolute an end as society can only be attained through a hierarchy or system of relative ends. Here the possibility of empirically demonstrable internal inconsistency is obvious. Second, a conservative bias will be unavoidable, for society has always favored some groups at the expense of others and "staying the same" must mean continuing to favor the same ones. But then, third, our original motive for adopting functionalism as a principle of explanation will be frustrated, for functionalism was to have provided a check on our introspection, a method for achieving objectivity, value-neutrality. The principle that society is homeostatic was to have served as the social-scientific analogue of the conservation laws in the physical sciences, rather than as a conservative manifesto, in which capacity it is, of course, theoretically irrelevant.

These puzzling consequences seem fatal flaws in functionalism. We should recall that we did not adopt the method by accident. If one attempts to explain romantic love as if it were a psychological phenomenon, then—so we argued—one is inevitably led to the recognition that the psychological facts involved are determined by a historically conditioned social institution. It is difficult to be candid about that institution when the institution itself prescribes a flowery lack of candor in the conduct of our intimate affairs. Love does not wear its meaning on its sleeve. Surely it is only accurate to say that the very nature of our topic dictated our functionalistic method of argument to us. If dysfunctional doubts now lead us to question the explanatory power of that method, it does not follow from this that our original choice of it was mistaken. Indeed, what other method could we have chosen?

The very difficulty in which we now find ourselves—the difficulty, namely, that we can neither retain nor discard functionalism—demonstrates that one may "choose a method of explanation" merely in a manner of speaking. It makes sense to speak of choosing a method for explaining a subject-matter only if one knows in advance what should count as explaining it, in other words, only if one has already explained it sufficiently to make it seem likely that all that is lacking is more of the same. We chose "What is love?" as the subject-matter of this philosophical essay just because we did not know what should count as explaining love. Were we to choose a method for explaining it, we could then be asked by what method we chose that method. Here would begin a regress which could only be halted dogmatically.

Functionalism seems not so much to have led us astray as to have stopped leading us at all, to have become a method for glossing over the facts instead of explaining them. We are left with a sense of aimlessness. No doubt we should re-examine the argument in the hope that the subject-matter itself, romantic love, may suggest its intelligibility to us.

§11 Society as Agent and Principle

Our general purpose is to construct a philosophical theory of the question, "What is love?" This is a theoretical problem, not a moral or practical one; that is, we want to state the truth, not to accomplish a good work. Accordingly, accuracy and objectivity are the ideals to which our problem commits us. In Part I, we concluded that romantic love is most accurately regarded as a social institution and "What is love?" as a sociological question. In Part II, therefore, we have undertaken to give "What is love?" a sociological answer. We employed the functionalistic method as a guide to objectivity, a check on the sentiments, on the biases we are obliged to profess as laymen. Using this method, we showed in §7 that love is a code or expressive mechanism, and in §9 we explained this code by showing its economic function.

Here we might have concluded the argument, were it not also necessary to account for certain well-known doubts about the social utility of the romantical code, doubts whose theoretical basis is as obscure as their moral force is undeniable. These doubts suggest that the explanatory power of the functionalistic method is limited, that when the method is applied to romantic love, at least, it produces not satisfying explanations, but tautologies and apologies for the status quo. In the last section, we presented four such doubts. We argued that they cannot be dismissed as merely expressions of uninformed lay sentimentality. We are left, though, with a nest of baffling problems. The doubting critic questions—persuasively—the objectivity of functionalism, but he provides no alternative method. His doubts appear to arise neither quite from within nor quite from outside the functionalistic perspective. He argues that functionalism is limited by a conservative bias, but if the only alternative is a liberal or some other bias, then theoretical social science is impossible. Such a conclusion, however, verges on the self-refuting.

Our task becomes, then, to understand how the debate between the functionalist and his critic is possible, how the same institution can be the object at once of social criticism and sociological explanation. The debate is not so much a debate within sociology as a debate about the nature and limits of sociological explanation. As such, it leads directly into the ontological concerns of Part III. Thus if romantic love is a social institution, then what love really is will be determined by what the "society" is which fosters that peculiar institution, and this is what the functionalist and his critic differ over.

In this section, therefore, we shall try to accomplish two tasks. First, we shall try to resolve the debate between functionalist and critic by presenting a conception of society which differs from theirs. We shall argue that both make the same assumption, though in different ways. Both assume, namely, that society is an object different from themselves, an object that stands outside their activities of investigating and passing judgment on it. This assumption, we shall argue, is false, and instead of asking which of their judgments is the more accurate, we ought rather to ask from where or by whom each judgment is made, thus shifting the emphasis of our inquiry from the object judged to the subjects judging. The object judged is society, a collective activity. We shall argue that the subjects judging should also be construed as collective activities, for the real debaters are groups, not individuals. When we examine the criticism each of these groups makes of the other, we shall see that each takes itself to be different from society only by making the error the other criticizes. We shall propose that both errors may be corrected by regarding society as not primarily an object at all, but rather an intelligent, purposeful collective activity, something suspiciously like a moral agent, a knowing and acting subject.

Such a proposal is, of course, "counterintuitive," which is to say, unfamiliar. Put forward as the solution to an abstract debate between abstract, cardboard figures, it will seem unpersuasive. Therefore our second task must be to show the concrete sense of it, to make it seem less contrived and obscure. We shall see that the key to this problem is a predictable prejudice: the reader will feel threatened by the concept of society as a collective subject. We shall try to show the concept's intuitive plausibility by exorcising this threat. The ontological implications of the concept are the topic of Part III.

Turning to our first task, the debate between the functionalist and his critic may be presented as an antinomy in the Kantian sense, that is, as a debate in which each party gives not only an apparently conclusive argument for his own position, but also an apparently compelling refutation of his opponent's right to maintain the opposite. As we saw in §9, the functionalist argues that romantic love is socially useful. Exactly what such an institution as romantic love is, however, is far from obvious. Functionalism is a method for discovering what such institutions are by determining how they are justified. Thus the functionalist may claim that even his critic has to assume that love is justified up to a point, for otherwise he would have no way to identify the institution he criticizes. Having in that sense and to that extent conceded the appropriateness of the functionalist's method, the critic cannot abandon it later, except arbitrarily. His doubts may demonstrate the inadequacy of a given analysis of love, but they cannot—in principle—demonstrate the dysfunctionality of the institution itself. Pursuing our Kantian analogy, the functionalist might be said to be a rationalist: he argues that there must be good reasons for love's apparent dysfunctions, even though we are as yet unaware of those reasons. Expressed as a substantive thesis, such a position may seem a tautology; but its purpose is methodological, and unless we suppose there are good reasons to be found, we are unlikely to find any.

So the critic cannot be reasoning objectively, for to be objective means to ignore one's doubts, swallow one's indignation over apparent wrongs, and continue to search for the teleological sense the institution must make. The critic, however, argues, as we saw in §10, that romantic love is socially harmful, for its consequences are harmful. He finds the functionalist rather like the faith healer, who claims that pain is imaginary, even though imaginary pains hurt just as badly as real ones. As soon as one points out that the functionalist's "good" reasons are not so good after all, the functionalist shifts his ground. Hence his objectivity lacks an object, or worse, possesses one in the currently prevailing distribution of social and economic goods. Again pursuing our Kantian analogy, the critic might be said to be a moral empiricist: what counts as evidence to him are his concrete feelings of wrong, and a justification that abstractly explains those feelings away is really no justification at all. The strength of the critic's position lies in what he substantively asserts, not in his method of defending it. There he seems essentially parasitical on functionalism.

Romantic love as an institution exists because of our collective choice of a way of life featuring mass production, high consumption, small families, shallow ties to friends and locality, and a certain extravagant rhetoric. That this is a collective choice is indisputable, since we manage to live together by means of it. The agency that chooses we have called "society," and whether or not society should be thought of as possessing some hidden reserve of wisdom that would justify its choice is what is being disputed here.

To understand the debate between the functionalist and his critic, it is important to remember that however one may think of "society" and whatever ontological status one may assign to it, the question of the social utility or justification of the romantical code is a question we direct to ourselves. Society must be justified in our lay terms, for the supposition that there are other terms, that there may be some sense in which society is justified to itself or to some social-scientific priesthood but not to us, is either meaningless or worse. (We introduced this problem at the end of §4.3; we shall consider it at length in Part III.) The sociologist aims to prove. Proofs exist by being communicated. A solitary individual may discover a proof, but it gains the logical force of proof through expert endorsement. Although on the one hand the sociologist's proofs are addressed to his fellow experts who alone can understand and appreciate them, on the other hand, "good," "bad," "right," "wrong," "just," and "unjust" are not technical terms, but the very stuff from which everyday life is made. Seemingly technical terms such as "function" and "dysfunction" ought not to conceal from us that either these terms are translatable into everyday terms or else the proofs offered are irrelevant. The functionalist must prove or his critic must disprove that romantic love is justified in the layman's sense of "justification," for otherwise their dispute will not be about the real world at all.

The functionalistic method is built around the concepts of socialization and social control. Here the functionalist makes a persuasive case indeed. These concepts imply that society as a whole is present in the consciousness of each individual member of society, sometimes in a form of which he is unaware, but sometimes in a form which he does and should and indeed must recognize. Thus the individual's sense of right and wrong tells him he should on occasion subordinate his own interests to the interests of the larger groups to which he belongs. In order to do so, he must take the point of view of the group, sometimes even of the largest possible group, society itself. This latent openness to social control is what distinguishes sanity from the various forms of mental deficiency or incompetence, for the mental defective is unable, as M'Naghten's famous Rule puts it, "to recognize the nature and quality of his acts."

If, now, society must be justified to us in our terms—as the critic demands—then, as we have seen, this means it must be justified as one of us might justify himself to the others, that is, as if it had a point of view and were a fellow moral agent who could be called to account for his actions. That is what "moral justification" means. What is at issue in the debate is the sense this demand makes, for the ontological claim implied is certainly dubious. The functionalist, on the other hand, treats society not as a fellow agent who can be called to account, but merely as an abstract principle of explanation. Moreover, if, as the concept of socialization implies, the individual's moral conscience is socially derived, then the critic possesses no independent basis, no Archimedean point on which he might stand to find society unfair and its institutions dysfunctional. This lack does not mean— so we may soften the judgment—that social criticism is impossible, but only that it is nontheoretical. When we shift our concern from the determination of the truth to the accomplishment of good works, then we shift ourselves out of sociology.

I characterized the debate between the functionalist and his critic as "antinomic" because both sides appear to be at once indisputably right and unquestionably wrong. The issue under debate seems unclear, indeed scarcely definable. The choice between treating society as a responsible moral agent, a collective subject, on the one hand, and drawing a sharp, uncrossable line between social theory and social criticism, on the other, is surely a Hobson's choice. Our Kantian analogy suggests that some shift in our point of view, in our conception of the object under debate and of the debaters, might perhaps resolve the antinomy. To pursue this suggestion, it may be helpful first to review the debate in an abbreviated form, as two four-step exchanges.

Here is the first:

Functionalist: Society is justified in having the institution of romantic love.

Critic: But this institution can be shown to be dysfunctional.

Functionalist: All such a criticism can show is that a certain definition of the institution is inadequate.

Critic: But that reply converts your position into a tautology.

Here is the second:

Critic: Society is wrong to have the institution of romantic love.

Functionalist: But how can you be sure the institution really is what you say it is?

Critic: I base my argument on yours. You give specific functions to an institution, the family, which you define by a general function.

Functionalist: But here you endorse categorically what I endorse only provisionally or for purposes of sociological inquiry, namely, the value of the family. This value judgment removes you from sociology altogether.

We have already observed that neither functionalism nor the criticism that is its inevitable sequel seems to result from a blunder or oversight. They seem instead to be stages through which the explanation of romantic love must pass. In our analysis of the debate, we began by thinking of the debaters as individual experts—the one a trained and objective sociologist, the other a trained and morally sensitive one—investigating a certain immense object, the social order, and arriving at conflicting conclusions. We took for granted the obvious difference between the investigator and what he investigates, although precisely that is what each of them challenges in the other. Thus the functionalist maintains that the moral standards which underlie the critic's indignation are inculcated by the very same society he criticizes, while the critic maintains that the functionalist's professed objectivity disguises the harsh voice of conservative social interests. We have already suggested that these individual investigators actually function as spokesmen for groups, groups each of which denies the other's claim to be independent of the society it investigates. This in turn suggests a shift in our own point of view through which—still pursuing our Kantian analogy—we may be able to resolve the antinomy. Instead of asking whether that immense object, society, engulfs these groups—as each claims about the other—we should rather ask whether we can regard society as doing for itself what they claim to do for it. If so, then the objectivity and moral sensitivity that these individual spokesmen express could be seen to be organizing principles of society itself, rather than merely of certain groups of sociological specialists.

We shall endeavor to establish this thesis first as it applies to each of our disputants individually, then as it applies to both together. We begin with the functionalist, to whom society is an object by being a principle, an intellectual instrument.

To the functionalist, society is a principle of explanation. Society's homeostasis is the social-scientific analogue of the conservation of mass-energy in the physical sciences or the process of evolution in the biological. Although one could regard the very existence of the sciences made possible by these principles as a verification of them, such gross "verifications" can serve at most the moral purpose of enlightening the superstitious. Given a scientific meaning, they become circular. One assumes the special role of objective social scientist by assuming that society is homeostatic: the assumption is not something one lives by, but something one investigates by means of. There "is" such a thing as society just as there "are" such things as natural selection and the conservation of mass-energy: none of the three is in any interesting sense an individual thing itself, but each provides a scientifically fruitful perspective upon everything.

The social order is an order of reasons or justifications. It exists only in its members, and it exists in them by giving a structure to their motivations. Thus there are throughout everyday life prescribed ways to think and behave and "official" reasons for those prescriptions, "things to say" about them. Romance abounds in examples: individuals are supposed to look forward to marriage, the officially approved reason for marrying is falling in love, and the thing to say about a newly engaged couple is "They're very much in love!" Functionalism prescribes that the investigator should discount the face value of this official morality, attending instead to what we collectively accomplish by means of it, to the officially unanticipated consequences or latent functions of our social institutions, beliefs, and practices. We must be careful to observe that in itself, as the example of romantic love abundantly proves, this is a wicked way to behave. Official reasons give themselves out as sufficient reasons, even when they are of the negative, "Don't ask" variety. We must also be careful to observe that official reasons with unanticipated consequences are defined by contrast with official reasons that are indeed sufficient, or whose consequences are well anticipated and clearly intended. The latter define what we mean by a "reason."

If, now, as the critic suggests when he accuses functionalism of a disguised conservatism, we apply the functionalistic method to functionalism itself—attending not to what the functionalist says, but to what he does— then we see that the functionalist does indeed treat homeostasis as if it were a self-justifying end. We are familiar with the criticism that this all-embracing end is merely a tautology, a tautology that the functionalist surreptitiously supplies with a content, namely, the existing social order, the status quo. But examine this criticism again. Lesser prescriptions, short-range goals, little ends in fact have no value in themselves, but derive their value from their contributions to the moral order as a whole. Where these contributions are unapparent, where institutions have unanticipated consequences, latent functions, then the functionalist declares—in effect, or by what he does—that their dependence on the whole of society ought to be clear, or at least ought to be clear to himself and his colleagues in the sociological fraternity. He uses what might be called "transparent" institutions as the standard by which to measure these opaque institutions. He claims that society creates its members, but since it creates them by telling them what will justify their actions, and since it tells some justifications only to him and his colleagues, he claims in effect that they as a group stand on an independent basis, an Archimedean point outside lay society. We see that the functionalist's agency, his investigator's objectivity, his selfhood-as-sociologist consists precisely in his refusal to accept official reasons at face value—except where their face value is their real value, except where they actually do reveal how lesser ends contribute to that largest end which is society. Judging him by what he does, then, we see that the functionalist can be taken implicitly to declare that society is a subject like himself, an agency whose self-awareness has the form of the demand that institutions be transparent, that its reason be manifest to it in its concrete actions, or that the largest end recognize its own work in the lesser ends that are the means to it. In short, the demand for transparency around which function-alism organizes itself makes no sense except as a demand society imposes on itself.

The critic's position is built on the functionalist's. It is in fact the reverse. The critic looks upon society as a system of power relationships, relation-ships in part justifiable, but in part unfair and wrong. He sees that such an abstract prescription as homeostasis exhausts its meaning in the concrete occurrences it produces, in the petty triumphs and humiliations of living men and women. If some of those occurrences are evil, then to that extent the abstract prescription is unjustifiable. He finds in that abstract prescrip-tion, then, not his own agency, but an alien *Diktat*—an object, thus, that he stands over against and condemns. This capacity for independent judg-ment is the moral agency the critic attributes to himself. To this condemna-tion of society's misdeeds, the functionalist objects that phenomena such as pervasive loneliness, broken families, and discrimination against women and the aged simply are not wrong in themselves, indeed are meaningless in themselves. These phenomena owe their significance to the larger ends— ultimately, to society itself—that they fail to bring about. They are, one might say, the injustices of justice itself, for nothing can fail morally except a good intention. By judging the social system item by item, the critic claims that he and his morally sensitive colleagues stand upon an inde-pendent basis, an Archimedean point from which they pass judgment on society. The functionalist sees that since items in a system owe their mean-ing to that system, there is no such Archimedean point. Judging him as we judged the functionalist—by what he does—we see that the critic implicitly attributes agency to society in just the sense in which he attributes it to himself and his colleagues, namely, as the refusal to find good what is not concretely realized as good.

The functionalist errs in assuming that society is an end that can justify itself in abstraction from its concrete realization in the self-conscious lives of laymen. The critic errs in assuming that anything smaller than society has the power to produce a social injustice. Each sees the flaw in the other's reasoning, but not the flaw in his own. If the agency, the subjectivity, which each implicitly attributes to himself and his colleagues is taken—as the other's criticism suggests—to be society's own agency and subjectivity, then their conflict and our antinomy can be resolved. We should think of society as an intelligent and responsible collective subject rather than as merely an object, merely an abstract principle used by specialists for theoretical purposes or merely a haphazard congeries of power relationships. Indeed, one may suggest that were society merely an object in either of these senses, then the origin and legitimacy of the activities of investigating it and passing judgment on it would be the darkest of mysteries.

"Society" is, of course, a word with many meanings, some of which we shall explore in detail in Part III. Here we have used it to refer simply to whatever it is the functionalistic sociologist studies. This—as the concepts of socialization and social control imply—is a moral order, an ideal, a prescription for the distribution of social and economic goods. We have found that we may resolve the debate between the functionalist and his critic by regarding this order as being alike constitutive of the investigator and of the object he investigates. Indeed, by combining the criticisms our debaters make of each other, we may sketch out a conception of society that the ancient Greeks would have found congenial. The moral order, we shall say, leads a life of its own, though each of our debaters is aware of only half of it. Society is neither justified nor unjustified in the institution of romantic love. Instead, we should think of society as the collective activity of justifying itself through this and its other institutions. So conceived, the ideals that are society's primary constituents are not passive, external objects, but powers endeavoring to overcome their own abstractness, to make themselves concrete as a social world. As social scientists and social critics, we look for these ideals in the everyday world they have made, but they themselves supply the standards and the energy with which we look.

And they are defined—so our sketch will continue—only in so far as we succeed in finding them. Love, for example (and we shall argue in Part III that love is far more than merely an example), is clearly an ideal, but an ideal that has no more meaning than we manage to give it in our everyday activities of loving one another, in that vast assortment of actions and communications we call "loving." It can hardly be claimed that these activities are self-justifying or, to say the same, that what they collectively mean is clear; we have a visceral sense that we mean by them far more than we ever manage to say or accomplish by means of them. Perhaps the greatest strength of this conception of society as a collective subject is its ability to clarify this feeling, for it implies that what we mean by these activities is in part undefined, undefined just because we have not yet succeeded in defining it. We are creatures of our own time: the further definition of what we mean by loving does not now exist in the clarity of the sociologist's specialized intellect nor in the critic's moral sensitivity. It simply does not exist yet, nor will it exist until the concrete activities of ourselves or our successors have brought it into existence. Here our conception of society dresses up a familiar idea in philosophical abstractions: the moral future is not yet, the standards by which our successors will someday rightly condemn us exist now only in our inner sense that we cannot quite manage to say in detail what our own standards are.

Our problem has been to determine how objective sociological inquiry and social criticism are conjointly possible, not to say how either might be better conducted, these latter being problems we must leave for experts in those activities. We have concluded by suggesting that the concept of society as a collective subject is the foundation of that possibility. This suggestion is far from clear. If indeed it provides an abstract solution to an abstract specialist's problem, that does not tell us how to think about it concretely, what to picture by means of it, how to schematize it. Certainly while each of us knows how to think of himself as an individual moral subject, to think of all of us as a collective moral subject seems strange and obscure. We shall consider in Part III the ontological problems raised by this hypostatization of society. In the remainder of this section, we ought to see what can be done to remedy its strangeness and obscurity.

How might we remedy them? Nothing is more familiar than to think of oneself as an individual. Once the subject has been brought up, each of us is certain that there is and could be only one of him, and each of us attaches the greatest possible importance to this fact. His inner life, his subjectivity, is the experience of this individual uniqueness, which he does not experience as a recherché metaphysical property, but as the moral self-assertion fundamental to being himself. To himself, thus, he is a subject, that before which the drama of his experience is played—what looks, so to speak, rather than what is looked at. To himself, therefore, he differs from every content of experience, society very much included. It is this deep sense of individual moral authority that the critic calls upon and that the concept of society as a collective subject is felt to menace. That concept seems to imply that the individual is not an autonomous subject at all, but an object some other subject knows. Society threatens to swallow the individual whole. Since to himself he cannot but be himself, he must find the concept of the collective subject entirely repugnant. The concept accordingly runs the highest risk of rejection.

Our strategy must be to try to convert this risk into opportunity. We must show the individual in each of us how society can inoffensively be said to be ingredient in, indeed, essential to his sense of himself as an individual, so that he can then find in the concept of the collective subject not the denial of his individuality but rather the clarification of it. In order to show this, however, we shall have to catch the individual in each of us off guard; we shall have to trifle with the moral sense at his core. This is an impertinence, and an advance apology is in order. The theoretical basis for this impertinence will be examined in §13.

The idea of invoking individual self-consciousness as a philosophical talisman goes back to Descartes, who found a bedrock certainty in his own self-conscious existence: he thinks, therefore he exists. He exists as a thinking thing—an individual thinking thing. To this postulate Kant objected that a thinking thing as such is not an individual. Subsequent philosophy has oscillated between these two poles. Rather than pursuing this debate in its familiar form, our strategy should be to undercut it. We know that the argumentative function of the functionalistic method is to check our introspecting by referring the terms of it to their enforced senses. In philosophical debates, one is supposed to be a thinking thing: such are the protocols of those debates. This protocol entitles us to suspect that the context in which individual self-consciousness is made an issue implicitly dictates the individual selves philosophers have become conscious of there, and that these denatured forms of individuality are abstracted from a more fundamental form in which selfhood and self-awareness are morally required and morally consequential.

In everyday life, as opposed to philosophical debate, the consciousness of oneself as an individual is a moral experience. That experience might be said to have three sides. The individual experiences himself as unique, as a subject, and as morally authoritative. There could be but one of him; that one is something that thinks, not merely something thought about; and that thinking one is entitled to pass judgment on his own actions and the actions of others. This experience of one's own individuality is always latent, seldom manifest. It arises when it is needed; we shall see later when that is. For now, we may observe that since uniqueness, subjectivity, and moral authority are three sides of the same experience, they should imply one another. How they do so is not obvious. Society as a collective moral subject has two of these properties, but not the third, uniqueness. When the individual fears being swallowed whole, made an object, stripped of ontological rank and moral authority, he fears the loss of his uniqueness. That property is thought to carry the other two. This is the fear we must exorcise—that is, we must show the individual in each of us that the uniqueness he so prizes is conferred upon him by the collective subject. Men define one another, and define one another as unique individuals: this is the social process we must elucidate.

Individuality is more easily praised than defined. Bishop Butler wrote that "Everything is what it is and not another thing." Simply by definition, everything, human or otherwise, is unique, a one-of-a-kind individual with infinitely many properties or characteristics. Humans experience their own individuality, but this self-awareness involves only a few of their properties. We are entitled to assume that fundamental among these must be the morally relevant ones, that is, those properties which determine how the individual ought to treat others and what treatment he may rightfully expect from them. These properties constitute what we shall call the individual's "social identity." Goffman writes,

> Society establishes the means of categorizing persons and the complement of attributes felt to be ordinary and natural for members of each of these categories. . . . When a stranger comes into our presence, then, first appearances are likely to enable us to anticipate his category and attributes, his "social identity"—to use a term that is better than "social status" because personal attributes such as "honesty" are involved, as well as structural ones, like "occupation."[45]

By definition, social identities determine prerogatives; that is, some identities are morally advantaged over others. Whites, for what is perhaps the simplest example, are morally advantaged over blacks, for in many situations, thoughtful, friendly treatment will be felt as a demand by the black and a concession by the white, even though both are fully aware it is the only decent way to behave. If—to make a mathematical metaphor—we think of a social identity as a location in multidimensional space, then in our society the dimensions of that space are—at least—age, sex, social class, and race, for these are the scales by which we require that everyone be measurable. Thus one cannot not have an age, a gender, a class position, and a racial affiliation, those properties by which one would be identified in a newspaper story and by which small children are earliest taught to identify themselves. In egalitarian societies, to be sure, the sensitive issue of class will usually be settled by implication; race functions as a dimension of identity primarily in multiracial societies; and one could add other empirical details, details that we must leave to the sociologists.

In order to determine how the individual's sense of his own individuality actually functions in everyday life, we have to begin with his social identity, for only after having identified him by age, sex, class, and race will we be able to assign other properties to him. More to the point, he himself is required to have this basic self-awareness, on pain of being thought "out of contact" and so not the possessor of a creditable self at all. He has a body, for example, but society determines how he "has" it, what use he may make of it, what say he may have in the preserving of its integrity. The prisoner's mind may wander, but his body is locked up. Small children's noses are cleaned by their mothers, and both infants and mental patients may be required to submit involuntarily to surgery.

Social identities, however, are general. The moral rules defining a social identity apply not to any individual as such, but to all individuals answering to the relevant description. Thus "twenty-two-year-old, white, middle-class male" is a general description of John, and a crowd of further specifications further determines how others ought to treat him—or anyone else like him—and how they may rightfully expect to be treated by him. Social identities mesh or interplay analogously to actors' roles in a play, a metaphor so excessively apt that it grounds a sociological subdiscipline, "role theory." The employer must have employees, the husband a wife, the celebrity a mob that recognizes him on sight. It seems both true and a clear implication of functionalism that society forms a social system—in other words, again to make a mathematical metaphor, that social identities should be closed under the operation of encountering. Thus when any two persons, no matter how widely separated in age, sex, class, and race, come into one another's presence, their social identities should prescribe how each should treat and rightfully expect to be treated by the other. (The implication is not that they necessarily will possess this information, but that it should exist and they should seek it out.) Indeed, this "closure" metaphor may be given a global significance, for human agreements determine the values of nonhuman things. Animals, for example, obtain rights only through human spokesmen. Thus even though we customarily think of an identity in less grandiose terms, a social identity may plausibly be taken to prescribe a world, a total distribution of emphasis.

Social identities are general, yet each of us is a unique individual who prizes his individuality and would react sharply and negatively to the suggestion that he is merely a stereotype. John claims there is no one else exactly like him. On its face, of course, such a claim is either trivial or morally indefensible, for whatever John might put forward in defense of it will be either morally irrelevant (for instance, his unique fingertip whorls) or applicable to others and so not uniquely his own. The observation that to be an individual means to be exactly like everyone else is a philosophical cliché.

On the other hand, the fact that each of us is taught to value his own individuality so highly and to react so sharply to the suggestion that his stereotypical social identity exhausts what there is to him suggests that individuality is not metaphysically guaranteed, but instead that society requires the individual actively to seek it—whatever it may be. This suggestion seems paradoxical, however, for society is the system of moral controls that regulates our relationships to one another. By definition, therefore, the individual's social identity is all he is entitled to claim from others. John is, after all, just another twenty-two-year-old, white, middle-class male. On the other hand, John, like the rest of us, inwardly thinks he is somehow special, thinks what he is cannot be exhausted by what others know of him, by his place in the settled, public world of enforceable rights and well-defined characteristics. That thought appears to be a good part, at least, of what the private, inner man, the real self, the face behind the mask of social identity actually amounts to. When John thinks there is no one else quite like him, he might be said to place himself over against his own place in the moral order or to assert that he as an individual transcends the social world; but in this thought, he seems to be doing only what society demands and others expect of him. To paraphrase Descartes, it is as if the moral order stamps upon him, like the mark of the workman impressed on his work, a deep and intimate sense of transcending that very moral order itself. Paradoxically, then, the individual's consciousness of his own individuality seems to be at once morally required and morally forbidden.

John finds his individuality by transcending the social world, and he transcends the social world by being a subject, the looker as opposed to the merely looked at. The Kantian tradition makes this transcendence seem even more paradoxical yet, for, according to the Kantians, the subject of experience, the transcendent ego, is empty, contentless. Who is the real John Beispiel and what is this individuality that characterizes him? John transcends his social identity, realizes there is more to him than being twenty-two, male, white, and middle-class. We have seen, though, that a social identity determines a total point of view, a global distribution of emphasis, in short, the world—at least, the world someone such as John is obliged to conceive. The world is everything, and the opposite of everything is nothing. Therefore John's innermost self-consciousness must be devoid of content, empty. And that is how John himself experiences it: not as a content, but as a form or activity—namely, as the activity of transcending the world, of not being any of the world's manifold contents. John is conscious of himself not as part of that mighty spectacle, the world, but as that before which the spectacle is displayed, a knowing subject rather than a known object. But—so the Kantians would have it—the contentless knowing subject is not uniquely John Beispiel nor anyone else. It is pure form, necessarily empty, undifferentiated.

This argument, however, robs transcendence of its moral significance. Surely the knowing subject cannot be contentless. After all, the world John distinguishes himself from must be a world he first identified himself with: he can put off only what he first put on, can transcend only what is in some sense himself. Transcendence, individuality, and subjectivity are negative ideas that owe their content to what they deny. The world John, the individual, stands over against must be his own world, the world of his social identity. Perhaps if we examine this world more closely, we can find the transcendence of the individual contained somewhere within it.

Now as we have defined it, John's social identity is a claim, and a legitimate claim upon others. John simply is a white, middle-class, twenty-two-year-old male, and whatever he himself may think about it, this general, sharable identity determines how he is entitled to interact with others, who will in turn possess their own social identities with respect to his. Thus John lays claim to what are demonstrably his properties by living through them, keeping his social place, meeting within a reasonable standard the obligations incumbent upon him as a person of such-and-such a description. If he did otherwise, if he seriously tried to transcend his properties by living through another social identity—by behaving, for example, like the dowager Empress of China—others would perceive him as mad. His social identity, thus, is both enacted and enforced, and not by John alone, but just as much by those with whom he interacts and whose identities depend reciprocally on his. He and they can dwell in a common world, can share confined spaces and perform cooperative tasks, can muddle through the elementary business of life together only on the basis of an agreement, a working consensus about who each is and what each owes to the others.

The individual claims to be himself by interacting with others. He is always at risk, for he can be only who they agree to let him be. They too, however, depend entirely upon him. To say this is merely to say that identities are functional, to say—as we saw in §4.2—that the identity one really has is the identity one can use to share time and space with others. John's secret fancies of being a great lover or a smart investor are harmless to himself and others alike until he lays his hand on his date or his wallet; then we shall see what he really is.

So identities are tested in face-to-face situations. We also saw in §4.2 that the agreements which define those situations are settled primarily by tacit negotiations, negotiations in which identities are claimed by giving off signals and granted by interacting appropriately or in role. As a rule, therefore, what is enacted and enforced in face-to-face situations is not so much the self-awareness of individuality as its significant absence. Thus we saw in §4.3 how the moral order aims to realize itself in the spontaneous thoughts and actions of its products, individuals. Ideally, everyone is supposed to know his place without having to be told. When someone does have to be told, all those present will tend to feel themselves embarrassed and threatened, for knowing one's own place coimplies being able to take the places of the others. When John's pranking friends tell him the shy and virginal Marsha is a call girl hired to help celebrate graduation, their back seat encounter should leave both equally traumatized. As this example suggests, however, agreements—definitions—usually guide situations with some flexibility. Goffman writes,

> Instead . . . of starting with the notion of the definition of the situation we must start with the idea that a particular definition is *in charge of the situa-*

tion and that as long as this control is not overtly threatened or blatantly opposed, much counter-activity will be possible.[46]

For as long as she can, quite possibly Marsha will place a flattering construction on John's impetuosity, and when what she in her innocence takes to be the definition of the situation has been stretched past the snapping point, what will be aroused in her is a sense at once of outraged individuality and outraged typicality: "You shouldn't treat a nice girl like me like that!" She feels she has been treated unfairly, and she calls down upon John standards of fairness she has every reason to think he too should acknowledge.

Ordinarily, the individual—here Marsha—fits into her social identity and so into her world like a hand in a well-worn glove, making her daily rounds, doing and suffering only what she more or less expects, thinking about anything else except who she individually is. Now and then, however, something may jar her loose from her stereotypical social identity. A death, a natural catastrophe, a religious inspiration, reading Kant, really experiencing an art work for the first time—there are many possible stimuli, and no doubt sometimes one reflects on one's individuality for no reason at all. We should remind ourselves, however, of our functionalistic theme: individuality as a psychic occurrence derives its sense and its substance from individuality as a social force, just as conspicuous consumption depends on money in the bank. Marsha is someone—*this* potent individual, *this* authoritative judge of her own and others' conduct—in relation to others who are also someones, individuals. Her individuality is the putative source of her social identity, of the roles or concrete situational identities in which she encounters others: that is its function. She becomes aware of it when others fail her, when their assumptions startle her, when the automatic acceptance that had given her a smooth ride from situation to situation abruptly stops. Then she is driven to think about who she individually is.

Society is present to the individual in the form of the face-to-face situation, a fragile, temporary collocation of individuals who depend upon one another's acceptance. Their mutual acceptance is the agreement that defines the situation. The situation may also be said to derive its legitimacy from its embeddedness in more enduring social forms: larger ideals find their local and temporary realization in it. This realization, however, is the only reality they have: when it fails, then they fail too. The individual falling back upon his sense of himself as an individual finds an identity authorized by these larger ideals, for his sense that he must have situations in which to be himself is in fact no different from their recognition of their own unreality as merely abstract. Marsha the nice girl appealing to John in the name of the ideal of respectability falls back upon an abstract sense of herself defined by that same ideal; what she appeals to in John has the same definition and the same abstractness. Out of our reverence for individuality, we are accustomed to thinking that the concrete individual bestows the authority, the ontological weight of his concreteness on ideals, abstract moral standards. When we observe him actually using that authority, however, we find its structure, definiteness, and form already given it by those same ideals.

Thus consider a gamier example. Let Marsha be a prostitute, and a shabby one at that. Marsha the whore will have a lower threshold of outrage than Marsha the nice girl. She can be pushed too far, of course, although when she is, she cannot appeal to a sexual honor long sold. Here we may easily construct a cliché occasion for one individual to cry out to another not in the name of particular rights established by a definite situation, but simply as an individual, *this* someone who stands at the center of the world.

Of course this is a cliché example. When Marsha says, "But put yourself in my place, how would you like it if someone . . . ," we can readily supply appropriate details, for what are suggested here are stock vignettes in which nothing is morally doubtful, but we know what the characters are supposed to think and what we are supposed to think about it. The frequency with which we massage our morality with fictional treatments of the theme testifies to how titillating we find prostitution's naked exposure of the individual. At this time, at least, we seem not to have invested the same cultivation of the dramatic imagination in other deviant groups, the aged, for example, or the mentally retarded.

Like the capacity for articulate speech, the human ability to put oneself in the other person's place, to take his point of view, to see him as another individual like oneself, appears only in historically conditioned forms. The individual inherits the language he speaks. Similarly, society equips him with ready-made moral perceptions and judgments, with as it were a vocabulary of conduct. He draws upon that inheritance to define his situations and the roles he plays in them, acquiring a social identity, rendering himself thus accessible to others, the locus of thoughts intelligible to them and actions relevant to them, for unless they can tell who he is being and therefore how he ought to be, they will not perceive him as a person at all. The madman's internal controls are unintelligible to others, and so they perceive him as a threat. The sane man's self-awareness, however, usually need not be conscious, for his own uniquely individual point of view is not what he looks at but what he looks out from. What he sees and others see that he sees is the finished world of his moral inheritance.

Functionalism is often accused of treating that inheritance as static, although of course it is not. Certainly there is moral progress, at least in the sense that in the past each generation has looked back with dismay at the evil ways of its predecessors. We credit this progress to individuals who have now and then had the courage and prescience to stand out from the crowd and blow the whistle on society. Therefore we revere individuality, each of us feeling that while he may not himself be a moral hero, at any rate he knows what moral heroism must be like and how to render homage to it. The concept of society as a collective subject, the idea that the individual's recognition of moral ideals is the work of those ideals themselves, seems to threaten this sense of the ultimate value of individuality. If indeed society creates the individual, then he seems powerless to rise to an independent and disapproving point of view.

To say that the individual is society's creature is to say that he is far more dependent on the approval or agreement of his fellows than we traditionally take him to be. When that agreement is not routinely forthcoming in routine situations, then he falls back upon himself. We have seen that he falls back on the same dependence on agreement, but in a more abstract form. That abstract form, however, is nothing in itself: it is defined by its function, which is to reconstitute agreement, another concrete situation. In other words, the moral struggle of the individual endeavoring to maneuver himself from one situation to the next and the activity by which ideals— forms of agreement—struggle to achieve concrete existence as the social world are the same activity. We routinely assume that moral standards enjoy an abstract, atemporal existence, unsullied by the dust and heat of everyday life. In that abstract existence, however, they are merely ineffectual.

We also routinely assume that the atemporal existence of moral ideals makes moral heroism possible. The prescient individual reaches out to them, for, so we assume, they exist as much (or as little) in the future as in the present or past. They justify his condemning the evil present in the name of what is to come. This assumption is entirely retrospective, however. The future as merely future is nothing, and therefore justifies nothing. Thus the drama of the abused whore—to revert to that—is an old story, and any thrills we still find in it reveal our private quirks, not our public morals. In order to revive its dramatic life, we must transport our characters and their situation back to those far-off days when prostitution was taken for granted, when the procuress would meet the coach bringing the country girl to London.[47] Now if John—Lord John, as we may imagine him—says, "How terrible that you whores should be so abused!" he sets himself up for the reply, "Oh, Sir, do I not please you?"—weeping; and if Marsha complains, she risks starvation or a beating. The characters are a function of their situation, so of their time. This is the agreement that brings them together. They violate it at their peril.

And yet it was wrong that whores should be so abused, and somewhere along the way from the late eighteenth to the late twentieth century, individuals—some of them heroic—did come to realize this. Those individuals had to translate their private visions into public actions, into a world of laws, police, social services, and economic opportunities where the abused whore is at least not a visible commonplace. A world, as the functionalist is quick to point out, is a biggish thing, much too large and complex for any single individual to envision in advance. When we try imaginatively to recapture those moments when our present conception of the individual and his rights was being made, we must be careful not to read the accomplishment back into the process. It is only in trashy romances that Lord John throws a protective arm around dirty little Marsha's shoulders and muses, "Somehow, I see a world where poor little country girls like you won't have to . . . (etc.)." In the real world, the heroic individual can disengage his self-consciousness from his time only in concert with others, for his life is a concretion of the ideals which make that time.

We can review in our own past the slow arising of our moral and political institutions. For example, we can trace the emancipation of women and the concomitant decline of prostitution from Methodism through the Victorian extension of dignity, decency, and the franchise to the laboring classes, through the Edwardian suffrage movement, and on into our own time (when we may judge that the movement is not yet finished). Those institutions and the ideals they embody may seem to us solid objects, Durkheimian things which we as individuals stand over against, but that is the measure of their accomplishment. We can interpret each of them as a partial definition of what the individual person is, what his rights are, and how he is entitled to defend those rights. Collectively, they make us unique individuals with well-defined situations in which to be ourselves.

The problem we have been examining is the uniqueness of the individual, or how individuality comes to stand over against social identity. We are trained to think of this self-awareness as a constant possibility; we introspect our own introspective independence of the social order. Functionalism offers a check on this apparent independence, a method for determining its conditions and evaluating its significance. Therefore we began with the individual where his presence is required, acting out his social identity in face-to-face situations, and we asked what might entitle or empower him to transcend this enforced sense of himself. We found that there is indeed more to him than others presently make of him, but this "more" is abstract and they share it. It does not exist yet, though it should. It is society, the collective imperative of seeking agreement, in a not-yet-realized form. The individual is more than "merely a stereotype," but the rhetoric of that formulation is thoroughly deceptive, for he seeks and ought to seek the recognition of his fellows, and they recognize individuals precisely through the types those individuals concretely embody. In this sense, the social order is as individual as its creatures. Its power is the power of legitimacy, the power to declare what is justified. It embodies itself only in order to transcend itself, and in its own name. The individual may condemn the present world with its solid sense of right and wrong, but this is an act of faith that only the future can justify. Thus we know that our institutions will be rejected, and rightly rejected, by our successors, but we cannot tell on what grounds, for as soon as the moral future becomes predictable, it has arrived. In the present, there is no sure and certain way to tell a moral hero from a nut.

Our purpose is to give a philosophical theory of the question, "What is love?" Our theory is philosophical, that is, we interpret the question to ask, "What is love really?" In this Part II of the argument, we have examined the sociologist's explanation of love as a social institution. We did this in order to determine the limits of this way of explaining love, not in order to make a contribution to sociology—our intentions are ontological, not sociological. The "society" that is the fundamental explanatory principle of sociology is a system of prescriptions. The individual becomes a member of society—or we could say simply "becomes"—by learning to respond to those prescriptions, that is, by learning what he ought to do and who he ought to be. We said that romantic love crowns our hierarchy of primary relationships. The primary by definition are those relationships through which the individual defines himself. Although he must define himself as only one small part of the vast social whole, nevertheless—and especially when he plays the role of sociologist—he can do so only because he knows the whole itself as a whole. Looking for the moment intuitively at the individual looking out at his world, if he is a knot in the network of primary relationships, love being the chief of them, if his loves in effect define him, then he must sense that what he means by "love" necessarily transcends any account that treats love as only one of many social institutions. He also identifies himself with or responds to all those institutions that are said not to be love, and the account must neglect or misrepresent those feelings of identification. Intuitively, then, "love" must be another name for society itself. That sense of the term necessarily escapes what sociology can give, for sociology can give at most an account of love as one of many means to society as an all-embracing end. A detailed explanation of love as an end and a subject will be the concern of Part III. There we shall see the positive basis on which this negative judgment of sociological explanation rests.

Part III
Inquiry and the Inquirer

§12 Invocations

Philosophy is the science of questions, that discipline which examines simply as questions the questions other disciplines try to answer. Therefore the philosopher ought to investigate ill-defined, troublesome questions, questions with a large significance, but an obscure, perhaps even a threatening logic. Such questions challenge our familiar methods for settling questions and our traditional division of intellectual labor. We may hope to learn something new from them.

Our purpose in this philosophical inquiry is to construct a theory of the question, "What is love?" In Part I, we examined the layman's characterization of love as a mysterious, inexplicable feeling and the layman's interpretation of "What is love?" as the question "Which feeling is it?" By definition, the layman's answer to "What is love?" is dictated by moral prescriptions, that is, "the thing to say" in answer to "What is love?" is determined by imperatives of action, not thought, by qualities persons are morally required to display to one another rather than by objectively evaluated evidence. Therefore the layman's answer might better be called a "response" than an explanation—redundantly, a scientific explanation. The psychologist too defines love as an emotion, but his answer to "What is love?" is governed by explicit standards of objectivity, standards promulgated and administered by the science of psychology. Thus the layman answers to an audience of laymen, who regard him as a social interactant rather than as a disciplinary colleague: different sets of controls govern the lay response and the psychological explanation. The layman's response is part, but only part, of the evidence the psychologist is required to account for in his explanation of love. The layman's response, on the other hand, will take account of the psychological explanation only in so far as popularized versions of psychological theories have come to color what laymen sense to be their moral obligations.

We turned from psychological to sociological theories of love on two interdependent grounds. First, love may be a feeling, but this feeling is defined by the actions it is said to prompt. Those actions in turn are defined by largely implicit moral rules, rules that can be made explicit only by using evidence based on collective rather than merely individual behavior. Second, love is said to be a particularistic emotion, an emotion felt by one individual as such for another as such. Here what counts as an individual seems to be determined by culturally relative social rules rather than by man's psychobiological makeup.

Psychology is a natural science, a science that tries to explain human behavior as a natural phenomenon. To the psychologist, then, "Which feeling is love?" means "Which part, capacity, or activity of the human animal is it?" Nature is the presupposed, all-inclusive whole whose parts natural scientists investigate and theorize about. Nature is not defined by their inquiries, but instead they assume that nature is well-defined independently of their inquiring—an assumption that makes inquiring possible. This assumption is articulated in the fundamental requirement of objectivity. Thus Bertrand Russell writes,

> The kernel of the scientific outlook is a thing so simple, so obvious, so seemingly trivial, that the mention of it may almost excite derision. The kernel of the scientific outlook is the refusal to regard our own desires, tastes, and interests as affording a key to the understanding of the world.[1]

The nature of the natural scientist, in other words, is accessible only to those who can assume that special attitude toward it which is the natural scientist's objectivity. Instead of an attitude, we may speak of an identity, for one communicates scientific information to someone else by tacitly informing him that one is someone who acknowledges what is the case regardless of his own likes and dislikes and expects the same from him. Such an identity is the product of what Berger and Luckmann call "secondary socialization." Behind it will stand the natural scientist's identities as citizen, lover, and family man, the identities produced by his "primary socialization." Behind these identities in turn will stand society, the moral order, as that which authorizes identities and establishes priorities among them. In wartime or a family emergency, for example, the scientist may be obliged to set aside his work in favor of what are thought prior obligations to his country or his family.

In Part II, we examined love as a social institution, a "social fact" in the Durkheimian sense. As social scientists—for we tried to reason as sociologists in Part II—we assumed that society is an all-inclusive whole, a social world. We called this assumption "functionalism." We assumed that society, like nature, is well-defined independently of our inquiring about it, and we made this assumption in order to make possible inquiring about it. We interpret this social-scientific objectivity analogously to objectivity in the natural sciences, for historically, the social sciences arose as attempts to extend to social reality those methods that had proven so successful in the investigation of nature. Nevertheless, these two concepts of objectivity cannot be altogether the same, for the social scientist is personally involved in what he is obliged to be objective about—society—in a manner and to a degree in which the natural scientist is not personally involved in what he is obliged to be objective about, nature. This difference becomes obvious when we consider that in order to explain objectivity in either set of disciplines, we must make use of concepts drawn from social science, such as identity, obligation, and socialization.

In each case, the all-inclusive whole that our interpretation of "What is love?" presupposed was not so much referred to or described as *invoked* or called forth, invoked as an object whose meaning and function is not to be explained but to be taken for granted in order to explain other things: its parts and features, or the means to it. We take natural phenomena such as feelings to be parts of nature, but we do not take nature to be part of anything. Similarly, society's institutions have their defining functions, but society itself has no function. Like nature, society simply *is*, and when we invoke its existence as the fundamental presupposition of social-scientific inquiry, we make a fundamental ontological commitment. We made, in fact, two such commitments, and we assumed that those commitments somehow exclude one another. Thus we assumed that if romantic love is not a natural phenomenon, not a feeling such as hunger, thirst, fear, or (perhaps) infatuation, not part of man's evolutionary heritage, then it must be a social phenomenon, a moral reality, part of that collective activity which is society. Beyond assuming, more or less tacitly, that they exclude one another, we left the relation between these two fundamental ontological commitments unexplored.

Fundamental ontological commitments enter scientific inquiry not as results or conclusions, but through methodological assumptions. They are invoked as the world—the necessary, well-defined whole that inquiry is presumed to be about and whose features inquiry aims to determine. Thus if we assume that romantic love is a natural phenomenon, then the question "What is love?" becomes "Which natural phenomenon is it?" and the order of inquiry is from vague initial conjectures about the emotions to a concrete identification of love as a well-defined part of a system of natural phenomena, phenomena whose natures and relations are established by the objective proof-procedures of the natural scientist. But we did not choose to pursue this psychological direction of inquiry. We found it more plausible to suppose that romantic love is a social phenomenon, indeed, an informal social institution. Thereby "What is love?" became the question "Which institution is it?'' and our inquiry proceeded from the vague evidences of Part I, the rhetoric of feelings and promises, to the concrete identification of love in §9 as a rhetorical code used as the bonding agent in marriages for the collective purpose of promoting an economy of high consumption and mass production. Thus we explained love by explaining which part of society love is. Using the proof-procedures of the social scientist, we found love within an ontological commitment we had already made, and we anchored its reality there.

Throughout the argument, whenever its movement has stalled, whenever we have encountered tautology, edification, dogmatism, partisanship—the pathologies of explanation—our strategy has been to reconsider the question we were asking. A form of questioning singles out a questionable topic against a background of unquestioned assumptions, and we reason that the unnoticed influence of the ground on the figure may be responsible for our having stalled. After concluding what love is in §9, we found ourselves confronted in §10 with dysfunctional doubts that led us to question both that conclusion and the functionalistic method by which we reached it. We examined that method and its fundamental assumption, society, in §11. We emerge from §11 with a conclusion and a suggestion. The conclusion is that society is a knowing and acting collective subject, even as we ourselves are individual subjects. The collective moral life, society, is its own reason for being, but it lives only in us. It trains us to distinguish ourselves as ends from ourselves as means, for this distinction is its own self-awareness. We have referred to this distinction as the distinction of primary from secondary relationships, but we could have referred to it as the traditional ethical distinction of dignity from price. The suggestion, then, is that since the individual is defined by his primary relationships, love being paramount among them, and since society creates the individual—and so also itself—through those primary relationships, love therefore must be not merely another social institution alongside the rest, but another name for society itself.

In the light of this conclusion and suggestion, we can see now that we interpreted "What is love?" in Part I and Part II to ask "Which object is love?", love being presumed to be part of some large, necessary object, some world—nature or society. In both cases, the background against which love and its world figure is our own activity of inquiring, the intellectual movement which passes from one topic to another, now stalling and now proceeding, in the endeavor to set itself over against a fixed and stable object, romantic love. From §11, we now surmise that love can appear before us as a stable object of inquiry, a well-defined institution, only by first being somehow ingredient in the activity of inquiring itself. So far, however, this is only a surmise. What it means to call society a "collective subject," how love enters into society's subjectivity, and what relation obtains among romantic love, society, and our own activity of inquiring into the question "What is love?"—these are the large questions that should occupy us in this Part III.

We made yet a third invocation. By calling philosophy the "science" of questions in the Introduction and by announcing that I intended to theorize and prove, I invoked that ideal which defines theory as opposed to practice, thought as opposed to action, explanation as opposed to its moral simulacra: edification, dogmatism, partisanship, exhortation. This announcement of the author's intentions awakens in the reader (I shall presume) the recognition of the force and legitimacy of that same ideal; and the reader, who has the advantage over the author here, scrutinizes the author's text for the stylistic clues that indicate whether or not he is really faithful to the intention he announced and the ideal he invoked. In a book, only the author is exposed and may be discredited, print being a unidirectional, feedbackless medium. We may recall, however, that indirect social interactions derive their meaning from what they would mean were their participants face-to-face, sharing the same time and space through whatever ideal defines their situation. Thus in face-to-face situations, identities are mutually confirmed and participants monitor one another's fidelity to promises. In this sense, accordingly, author and readers here might be said to have invoked the ideal of theoretical objectivity together; that is, the invocation can be taken to be a collective action.

In itself, this third invocation does not seem to have any ontological implications. Until we say what we intend to theorize about, we do not seem to have invoked a world, a primary framework, a way of being real, and our objectivity does not seem to have an object yet. However, §11 suggests that this omission is only an appearance, that we have already made a fundamental ontological commitment through our collective invocation of the theoretical ideal. After all, our most fundamental ontological commitment is to ourselves. We must concede, therefore, that we ourselves are real in our mutually granted identities as inquirers. The test and the life of an ideal is its legitimacy, its power to create enforceable identities, its ability to enlist men in its service. We have attested to the power and legitimacy of the ideal of theoretical objectivity. That attestation, that mutually promised subjectivity, is the ground against which our argument has figured.

Considered just in the abstract, this invocation of the theoretical ideal makes no direct ontological commitment. The commitment it makes is indirect, or lies in what it takes for granted, namely in the potent tradition of free inquiry that makes it possible. By inquiring, we tacitly declare that inquiry is a good activity and that we are justified in being inquirers. We assume that society is the silent, approving witness of what we do and who we are, the ultimate agency which authorizes inquiry and the inquirer and in whose name we act.

Our third invocation, then, was of society as the chief good, the ultimate source of moral authority or legitimacy. There is no Archimedean point outside society from which society could be judged. Thus Aristotle writes that the determination of the chief good

> . . . would seem to belong to the most authoritative art and that which is most truly the master art. And politics appears to be of this nature; for it is this that ordains which of the sciences should be studied in a state, and which each class of citizens should learn and up to what point they should learn them; and we see even the most highly esteemed of capacities to fall under this, e.g. strategy, economics, rhetoric; now, since politics uses the rest of the sciences, and since, again, it legislates as to what we are to do and what we are to abstain from, the end of this science must include those of the others, so that this end must be the good for man. For even if the end is the same for a single man and for a state, that of the state seems at all events something greater and more complete whether to attain or to preserve; though it is worthwhile to attain the end merely for one man, it is finer and more godlike to attain it for a nation or for city-states.[2]

Accordingly, society is invoked in the argument in two ways: through our explicit invocation of the tradition of objective inquiry in the social sciences, and through our tacit assumption that inquiry is a legitimate activity we may honorably pursue. Neither invocation is dispensable, for without the former, the argument would lack an object, and without the latter, it would lack its right to be. In the dysfunctional doubts of §10, these two invocations might be said to have come into conflict, and so we discovered in §11 that the argument is not entitled to undercut its own justification, that is, that we are not entitled to discover of society that it is merely a coincidence of amoral forces, a mindless power that could not justify anything, including and especially our own activity of inquiry. Such a "discovery" would be tantamount to declaring that sociology—for the argument of §10 is sociological—is self-justifying, that the sociological community stands on an Archimedean point outside of the larger society which trains, supports, and rewards sociologists and whose presence within them gives their science a subject-matter.

The community of social scientists, like the community of natural scientists, exists within the larger society that legitimates both. It follows that we may speak of three invocations and three rival fundamental ontological commitments only in a preliminary way. In the light of §11, our invocation of society as the authorizer of inquiry must incorporate our earlier invocations of nature and society as objects. Thus by analogy, one can

106

point to an object within one's visual field, but one cannot point to the visual field itself: the visual field is as it were the objective correlate of the activity of pointing. Similarly, nature and society as necessary objects or worlds are nothing in themselves, but exist only relatively to those activities of explanation that are the natural and social sciences: they are the objective correlates of the activity of inquiring.

We should shift our attention, then, from nature and society as objects and from love as part of them to the activity of inquiry itself and to the objectivity that defines it. What is the place of inquiry within that all-encompassing and self-justifying activity which is society? How does objectivity in the natural sciences differ from objectivity in the social sciences? Society is a collective subject, an ideal justifying itself by organizing humans through institutions. Romantic love is one of those institutions, but we surmise that love is also another name for society itself. By examining the two lesser ideals of objectivity, we may be enabled to name the largest, encompassing ideal that legitimates them, and we may be able to determine the relation of love to that ideal. Here we raise a problem similar to what the medieval Jews called the problem of the "names of God." Spinoza writes,

> Furthermore, we must note that Jehovah is the only word found in Scripture with the meaning of the absolute essence of God, without reference to created things. The Jews maintain, for this reason, that this is, strictly speaking, the only name of God; that the rest of the words used are merely titles; and in truth, the other names of God, whether they be substantives or adjectives, are merely attributive, and belong to Him, in so far as He is conceived of in relation to created things, or manifested through them.[3]

The Jews maintain that Jehovah, Jahweh, the Tetragrammaton alone names God. This is His proper name, presumably because He chose it Himself (Exodus 6:3), rather than a description ranking Him alongside of or in relation to His creatures. By analogy, then, our problem becomes to determine society's proper name and the relation of love to what that name names. We shall conclude by solving this problem.

§13 Objectivity as a Social Process

In the preceding section, we observed that fundamental ontological commitments should not be said to be described or inferred, but rather to be invoked, called forth, named. They are not results of inquiry; they are the *archai* or starting points which make inquiry possible. When scientists gather in the laboratory or when a reader begins some author's *Principles of Physics*, the ground—nature—on which these encounters will figure has been prepared in advance. Laboratory team, author, and reader already know who they are and what they are doing. They stand from the beginning over against a massively necessary object, a world—a world they assume well-defined independently of what they do together and say to one another. Nature is not affected by their reading, writing, and experimenting. Instead, nature is thought to be the ground against which they communicate or the arena within which their intellectual encounters take place.

We said we made three such invocations. We invoked nature and society as ultimate objects of inquiry, and we invoked society as the ultimate moral authorizer of inquiry. We suggested also that the third of these invocations incorporates the first two, for by assuming that we are entitled to investigate love as a psychological and social phenomenon, we find our own identities as inquirers within the activities of psychological and sociological inquiry and we implicitly commit ourselves to the existence and identity of the authority that legitimizes both these activities and the worlds that are their objective correlates. Our problem in this Part is to understand how these three invocations are related to one another and how love is related to the third of them.

The troublesome word "society" is used in many ways, two of which have been especially important to our argument. In one sense—a lay, intuitive sense—"society" is a way of referring to all of us, and all of us are clearly more important, valuable, and morally authoritative than any one of us. Society in this sense is that to which the convict must pay his debt and to which those with unimpaired moral, mental, and physical faculties may make a contribution. In another sense, a sense derived from the functionalistic tradition in social science, "society" is that agency which preserves itself by socializing us and by organizing us through institutions. We saw in §11 that the second sense is derived from the first, for "transparent" institutions make an understood and acknowledged contribution to the social whole, and what the functionalist shows is how other phenomena also contribute, but in obscure and hidden ways.

Something, then, not only persists but ought to persist through our efforts, something somehow identical to all of us collectively. One name for this ultimate, prescriptive entity, this living ideal, is "society." In this Part, our problem is to identify the collective moral life more concretely and defensibly that we do with this name or with such scattershot adjectives as "ultimate," "collective," and "moral."

The analogy with the theological problem of naming God is entirely apt and indicative of the magnitude and nature of the problem. "God is love," says the Bible (I John 4:16). We approach the problem through the secular disciplines of philosophy and sociology, therefore with a paramount commitment to objectivity. Even from that objective vantage point, however, we have seen that we use the distinction of primary from secondary relationships to distinguish the individual as himself, an irreplaceable element in the social process, from the individual as a dispensable economic counter, and that romantic love crowns our hierarchy of primary relationships. The romantical code is a concrete historical institution that makes a definite and not altogether positive contribution to society. We saw in §11 that we can account for both the positive and the negative elements in this contribution by supposing that society is a collective subject and the institution as it were the best society has been able to accomplish up to now. We have the suggestion, then, that love is somehow identical to the social process itself, so that when we as laymen shield love from definition and explanation by calling it a feeling, society speaks through us to declare its own ideality and indefinability.

Society is an individual, an ideal, and a subject. The language has a *feierlich* ring which invites misunderstanding. We should recall the argument of §11, however. Each of us thinks of himself as an individual, a subject, a being who transcends his own social identity and whose existence cannot be exhausted by any description. Individuality is reciprocal, for individuals accredit one another. Ontological commitments to individuals, therefore, are based on naming them rather than describing them. Who is the tallest man in the regiment, or who is the regimental sergeant-major? "John Beispiel." Naming John credits him with an existence transcending these or any other descriptions. And we name him out of our own names: by naming him, we point to him, but we point from where we are, and on condition that he point back. As we saw in §11, we appeal from formal systems of social rank to a reciprocity presumed morally prior and constitutive of individuals as such. We say, "But put yourself in my place," "Look at it from my point of view," and the like, summoning up in one another a self-consciousness which is neither individual nor collective alone, but in which these two moments are functions of one another.

An individual as such can only be named, not described. We noted in §11 that reciprocity, the human ability to put oneself in the other person's place, to take his point of view, to recognize him as another individual like oneself, appears only in historically conditioned forms. We can say either that each of us recognizes the exercising of this ability as the most fundamental of his obligations, or we can say that this ideal brings about its own existence by creating for itself a world of persons who recognize it as the most fundamental of their obligations. The two formulations are equivalent, the first emphasizing the dependence of the individual on society, the second the dependence of society on the individual. Because this ability appears only in historically conditioned forms, it is an individual object. But because, as §11 argues, it transcends each of those forms in the same way each of us transcends his own social identity, it is accordingly an individual subject, as it were a collective individual subject. Our problem, then, is to name our own society, to name what we take to be our highest ideal or our most fundamental obligation; or, reversing the formulation, our problem is to name that ideal of which we are the instruments and the outcome.

The awesome superlatives we are forced to use even to state this problem suggest that its solution must lie far beyond the reach of such a theoretical discipline as philosophy, perhaps in the realms of faith or fantasy. No doubt we should not hope for too much. We do know at least this, that we ourselves are together as we pose the problem of naming society, that highest ideal which holds us together. We have committed ourselves to the proposition that whatever ideal society is, we forward that ideal through inquiry. When we say society is a subject, we must mean at least that it is what we are, and we do what we are now doing—theorizing, reasoning together—by granting one another concrete identities or by ourselves being particular subjects. Society authorizes our objectivity. If, then, we can construe that objectivity itself as a social process, we may hope to find in it some clue to the identity of the larger social process of which it is only one legitimate part.

Historically, the natural sciences have provided the baseline of objectivity, the simplest, clearest experiences and principles that established the meaning of the term. Because we know that and how objectivity is possible in the natural sciences, especially in physics, we can subsequently ask whether and how objectivity is possible in the social sciences. In considering objectivity as a social process in general, therefore, we should concentrate first on objectivity in the natural sciences, leaving those problems peculiar to social-scientific objectivity for the next section.

Proof is one of the many forms of communication, one of the many ways in which one individual can intentionally take upon himself before others the responsibility for influencing their thoughts and actions. We saw in §4.2 that explicit communication presupposes tacit, identity-establishing communication. Thus before a message can be received, the sender must inform the receiver who each of them is to be taken to be and in what spirit or light or frame of reference the message is to be received. Where communication is expressly intended to convey information rather than to influence actions or attitudes, where its official object is to state the truth, a world is invoked, and along with it the special identities that must be assumed by those who wish to exchange information about that world. We have seen that nature and society are two such worlds, universes of discourse accessible only to those who are prepared to be objective. We may recall our earlier quotation from Russell:

> The kernel of the scientific outlook is a thing so simple, so obvious, so seemingly trivial, that the mention of it may almost excite derision. The kernel of the scientific outlook is the refusal to regard our own desires, tastes, and interests as affording a key to the understanding of the world.

Such an outlook, such an attitude may seem obvious and trivial, but it is not simple. Attitudes and identities are actions, and therefore are open to moral judgment by others. To assume an identity—that of objective inquirer, say—means to project role-relevant identities into those with whom one interacts in that identity. This is the mutuality or reciprocity we use the dramaturgical metaphor to elucidate. Identities thus define obligations that may not be kept and expectations that may not be fulfilled. They have a promissory quality. We view the enormous fact that is nature through the lens of scientific objectivity, but that lens, that mutually agreed-upon distribution of emphasis or mode of interpretation, is invoked, as we may say, ceremonially, where a "ceremony" is the manifest public acknowledgment of a moral ideal, the open mutual underwriting of a code. The kernel of the code may seem simple—we shall examine the point shortly—but the code itself, like any other moral fact, has its lengthy history and its present existence in a welter of partial and qualified forms. For example, objective inquiry may be qualified by the obligatory pieties of the political or religious organization that authorizes it, as are economics in communist nations, biblical archaeology among fundamentalist denominations, and, disputably, the study of the inheritability of intelligence in our own country. Wartime invariably produces "objective" studies that we later recollect with embarrassment. In cases such as these, objectivity operates under a limited franchise. To say that in itself objectivity admits of no limitations is another way of declaring that nature is all there is.

Nature may be all there is, but one can come to know about this all-inclusive whole only by joining one of those well-defined social groups that are the natural sciences, if only in the humble capacity of complaisant layman. Goffman writes,

> Social groups, whether big or little, possess some general organizational properties. These properties include regulation of entering and leaving; capacity for collective action; division of labor, including leadership roles; socialization function, whether primary or adult; a means of satisfying personal ends; and latent and manifest social function in the environing society.[4]

A social group is a moral entity, a collective response to an ideal. As Russell indicates, the kernel of that ideal whose power to elicit collective action and provoke shared sentiment manifests itself as the natural sciences is objectivity, the refusal to regard one's own desires, tastes, and interests—all that sets one apart as one individual among others, all that gives one a social identity—as affording a key to the understanding of the natural world.

This negative definition has a positive coimplicate, namely, that ideal which defines "proof" in its most fundamental and authoritative sense, the ideal of universal assent. A proof, we say, should be "capable of compelling universal assent." The cliché example is the "two plus two equals four" of arithmetic. Indeed, because this ideal is most nearly approximated to by mathematics and the more readily quantifiable natural sciences, we call them "exact sciences." Art criticism, by contrast, is notoriously inexact, although critics do make judgments and do endeavor to substantiate those judgments. We hesitate to dignify those substantiations with the honorific title "proof," but this hesitation only testifies to how much they deviate from the ideal that nevertheless defines them. The critic addresses a limited, specially qualified audience, to be sure, but he must regard that audience as in principle capable of indefinite enlargement. If he did not, then his "proofs" would be merely exhortations: they would be intended to foster an in-group solidarity, not to demonstrate. The critic's audience of cognoscenti differs from the public at large, however, not through conversion or divine or aesthetic election, but instead through a knowledge of the arts and a cultivated taste, and in principle, the public could be taught and cultivated.

Accordingly, the ideal of universal assent realizes itself in the form of groups of persons who collectively agree to abide by it, submitting their judgments to the discipline of proof. These social groups are made possible by the same social processes, namely recruitment and retirement, division of labor, allocation of rewards, repression of disruptive hostilities, and in general, the same disciplined subordination of individual passions and interests to a larger collective end. In short, objectivity is the object of special forms of social control.

As the term "objectivity" itself indicates, the natural sciences are directed away from themselves and toward their common object, nature. The social processes that make them possible as ways of knowing or agencies of proof are expressly designed to insure this other-directionality. It is achieved more easily in some sciences than in others, more easily in physics and chemistry, for example, than in biology. Electrons and mass-points, ions and valence bonds, are not lures for feeling. The neophyte biologist dissecting the proverbial cow's eyeball, however, will have powerful feelings that he must learn to repress. Primary socialization has given him a healthy respect for the integrity of the body, a deeply habitual response to the body as a symbol of the sacredness of the person. He must repress the threatening feeling that the eyeball he slices open might be his own or some other living person's, for this is what his automatic feelings of sympathy tell him. The cow's eyeball is an object—an abstract object, in fact, for he dissects this particular eyeball in order to learn about all eyeballs—and he is a knowing subject sharing a laboratory hour with other knowing subjects. His person, his status as a creditable member of the moral community, depends upon his ability tacitly and unthinkingly to assure others that he can be counted on to respect their bodies and counts on them to respect his. Of course this painfully elementary question is assumed to be settled before he enters the laboratory, or indeed, for that matter, before he is allowed to roam around on the loose. The laboratory with its elaborate ceremonial, embedded as it is in a university, the university in turn in the community, points him away from himself and his everyday relations to others. It tells him how to disengage himself, his feelings, from the eyeball he dissects by telling him how to degrade it into an abstract object in a general theory, a universal of which the squishy thing he slices is merely an instance.

Ordinarily, we think of objectivity as a moral posture obligatory for the individual inquirer. Objectivity is obligatory for the individual, however, because it is first of all a principle of social organization, an ideal around which groups can form. The individual inquirer implicitly promises his fellows that he will set aside his desires, tastes, and interests—those qualities, activities, and sensitivities by which he ties others to him with bonds of affection—for the purposes of the inquiry, and on condition that they do the same for him. The importance of individual derelictions lies in their threat to the group itself as a social process, a mutual or reciprocal accommodation of judgments, an expression or realization of the ideal of universal assent.

In general, a judgment, attitude, or inquiry is said to be "objective" if it is nonpartisan, unbiased, disinterested, in short, uninfluenced by the merely private concerns of the individual or individuals whose judgment, attitude, or inquiry it is. Objectivity in this general sense is a prerequisite for any intelligent, cooperative use of information. We are concerned with that special form of objectivity called "scientific" or—more appropriately— "theoretical." The concept was first clearly formulated by Aristotle.[5] An inquiry may be motivated by curiosity alone. Its purpose may be to acquire knowledge for its own sake. If so, it is a "theoretical" inquiry. On the other hand, it may have, or also have, some moral or utilitarian end, and in such a case, it is less than theoretical. (In idiomatic English, it is more customary to distinguish "pure" from "applied" science, or "science" from "technology," so that "theoretical science" becomes a redundancy.)

If we think of a (theoretical) science as a body of actual and potential information, then whether the individual scientist is engaged in a genuinely theoretical inquiry or in something less will depend on the purity of his intentions. If he wants to add to the body of scientific information merely for the sake of doing so, then he acts as a genuine theorist. On the other hand, if he wants, or also wants, to win a war or a promotion or a Nobel prize, then his inquiring activity is less than theoretical. When we think of the concept of theory in this familiar way, treating it as a standard of purity for individual intentions, we often find it awkward to apply, for intentions are notoriously elusive, sometimes eluding even the intender himself.

On the other hand, if we think of a science not as a body of information but as a social group, and of theoretical objectivity not as an individual virtue but as a social process, then the concept of theory becomes more perspicuous and manageable. Such a social group as a science must sustain its sense of collective identity by meeting from time to time. A meeting requires agreement over two matters: a topic or focus of interest, and a way of dealing with that topic. The first determines rules of relevance, rules that prescribe what information ought overtly or officially to be noticed by participants; the second determines rules of procedure, rules that prescribe how they ought to behave. The members of the group define the meeting as a face-to-face situation by tacitly promising one another to abide by these two sets of rules. The sincerity or insincerity of these promises is hidden within the promisers, but the promises themselves are public facts, and may become manifest public facts should someone be thought to have broken a rule.

During an experiment in chemistry, some topics are thought relevant, pertinent to the business at hand, fit to be mentioned, while others are thought irrelevant, out of place, disruptive. Topics of the first sort are "chemical" by definition. Topics of the second include, among other things, the social and personal identities of the chemists, their public positions and private loves, and—especially—their feelings of affection or hostility toward one another. Rules of procedure are largely prohibitory. Save for instrumental purposes, chemists should not touch nor even draw too near to one another. Loud noises are inappropriate and the pace of movement and speech should be unhurried. Affect must be carefully controlled, and overt displays of physical need are forbidden. Delicacy is, of course, a delicate matter: the rules will incorporate permissible exceptions, provisions for emergencies, and many other complications.

We want to understand how the ideal of theoretical objectivity realizes itself by means of the rules of propriety that define theoretical social situations. Here an analogy may be useful. Experimental scientists use the results of experiments conducted at particular times and places to draw conclusions about what is true at all times and places. The process of reasoning involved is called "induction." Analogously, particular individuals engage in theoretical inquiry together and arrive at results claimed to be valid for everyone, not just for them. One must have a location in order to be an experimenter and one must have a social identity in order to be a theorist, yet the conclusions of the inquiry transcend the identities of the inquirers just as the conclusions of the experiment transcend the locations of the experimenters. In both cases, one may ask how this is possible. We are accustomed to posing the problem of induction as if what is problematical is the individual experimenter's right to infer anytime, anyplace laws from sensations he as an individual has at some here and now. In fact, however, the laboratory is a social place. The sensations of the individual experimenter count as sensations only under the assumption that he is not drunk, hallucinating, or the like. Induction is the same logical process whether the sensations generalized upon are had by a single individual or by a laboratory team. Indeed, the team is logically prior, for the individual's sensations count only under the assumption that a team might have had them. In this sense, the analogy is more than merely an analogy.

The bodies chemists inhabit and the information about one another they possess are the same when the chemists meet to conduct an experiment and when they meet to plan the annual laboratory picnic. In the first case, they reach conclusions for which they claim universal validity. In the second, they merely advance the interests of their particular group. The proprieties must make the difference. Pursuing our analogy, then, just as the logic of induction tells the experimenter how to discount his particular spatiotemporal location even while he occupies it, so the social organization of theoretical inquiries, the rules of relevance and conduct, what they tacitly promise one another to attend to and ignore, and how they tacitly promise one another to behave must enable inquirers to discount their own particular identities, even while possessing them.

The kernel of the theoretical outlook is the truism that the truth is no respecter of persons. Their particular desires, tastes, and interests afford no key to the understanding of the world. We may enlarge our understanding of Russell's principle, however, by asking what they do afford a key to. Here the answer is plain enough: social relationships among persons. They define the individual's subjectivity. They are the sensitivities by which he attracts others to himself and by which they in turn attract him. Our desires, tastes, and interests afford no key to the understanding of the world because the world is indifferent to our relations of social superiority or inferiority, affection or hostility. And that defining principle of objectivity must manifest itself through the theoretical proprieties.

Chemists engage in chemical experiments as particular persons. They come together in the laboratory having knowledge of one another, bearing relationships to one another. The process of inquiry—an experiment, for example—takes time. During this time, individual interests will be advanced or retarded, friendships formed, antagonisms provoked. This untheoretical moral activity never stops. But this unceasing activity is surreptitious, clandestine. We know it happens inevitably, but we also know we are not supposed to pay attention to it, except perhaps to rebuke it. We know that the rules of relevance rule out paying attention to information of a personal nature, even while we busily exchange this information. The function of the rules is not to stop this exchange—as if such a feat were possible—but to keep it officially suppressed, to damp it down and take the sting out of it. For example, we enforce the basic rule of procedure that one should keep one's distance, for important changes in social relationships are symbolized by penetration of another's physical space. Chemists enter the laboratory related to one another in various ways. They know their relationships will change during the course of their experimenting, perhaps only slightly, perhaps more than slightly. The rules of propriety maintain the fiction that their relationships are not changing, even though the chemists themselves know otherwise.

By definition, every social situation is bounded by rules of propriety requiring some relationships among participants to be held constant during the time of that situation; otherwise, participants would have no way to distinguish that time from other times differently organized. Here theoretical situations represent an important extreme, for all of the participants' social relationships are supposed to remain unchanged throughout the situation and regardless of its outcome. The members of the group use the presumed and obligatory impersonality of their relations to one another to signalize to one another the indifference and implacability of the facts they confront. But since those relations are personal—they are, after all, relations among persons—the most that can be done with them is to leave them alone, as it were to put them on ice. By collectively enforcing the fiction that the time of those situations is socially static, we separate theory from practice and make theoretical situations fit for the pursuit of knowledge for its own sake. Immobility of social or primary relationships within the group is the schema for the ideal of objectivity that defines theoretical activity, using "schema" in the Kantian sense for a procedure of imagination that makes possible concrete application of an abstract rule.

It seems worth stressing that theory is a fragile activity. The truth may be indifferent to the fate of humankind, but men themselves are more sensitive. They can collectively agree to sustain a socially static time only if each of them is reasonably confident of being sustained by the others. Here the proprieties do their work, providing a vocabulary of signals that inquirers may exchange in order to promise one another that they can be trusted to leave persons and personalities out of the theoretical business at hand. We overlook too easily what a sophisticated ritual this is. It has no ground in nature—far from that, our concept of nature would appear to be grounded in it. Historically, it is a recent invention. Any major dislocation such as a war or revolution tends to pervert it. Children are too young to participate in it. Indeed, a long apprenticeship is required to train the scientist how to define himself and his fellow theorists as persons who can be trusted to seek the indifferent truth by putting their personal interests aside.

Reviewing our argument: Objectivity requires the theorist to attend to his object as it is in itself regardless of whether or not he is attending to it. We think of him as an active, practical being with interests to advance, interests that influence his attention. He is to take an interest in the object, then, regardless of whether or not the object advances his interests; that is, he is to have a certain motivation. Interest, attention, and motivation, however, are internal to the individual, factors in that mind to which he is presumed to have a privileged access. Objectivity at this level of analysis governs a transaction between the individual and his conscience, and there seems little one can usefully say about it.

Our next step was to put this abstract requirement of objectivity into context by putting the theorist upon whom it is imposed into his social context. He is someone trained to respond to it, someone therefore who has satisfied his trainers that he is properly trained—someone who, whether or not he actually has the required purity of motivation, can at least convince others that he has it, or has a sufficient degree of it. So we observed that objectivity as an achievement of individual self-discipline is made possible by conventions, by proprieties that permit this achievement to be publicly displayed for the acceptance of others in face-to-face interaction. Accordingly, the individual theorist is the subject of objectivity only derivatively, for he imposes this requirement upon himself in concert with others— immediately with his disciplinary interactants, through them with the discipline itself as the institution that licenses or authorizes particular face-to-face interactions. We may recall Goffman's statement that "ritual work is a means of retaining a constancy of image in the face of deviations in behavior." The fundamental subject of objectivity is neither the individual theorist in his privacy nor the particular face-to-face theoretical group, but the disciplinary self-image the group projects by means of the proprieties. This will be the image of a corporation of idealized, interest-free observers, pure spectators in whom action is entirely subservient to thought. The activity of projecting this collective self-image is the corporate life of the discipline—a dependent life, as we have seen, for the discipline exists on society's sufferance. We asked next how the proprieties allow the individual to display his dutiful participation in the projection of this collective self-image. Here we argued that rules of relevance and procedure enable theorists tacitly to promise to one another that none of them need take an interest in himself as a social being, for theoretical time is to be socially static; the individual may therefore safely attend to the object of inquiry alone. Immobility of social relationships within the group functions as the schema for objectivity by guaranteeing that the social consequences of the group's own commingling shall not be problematical for them. Since this guarantee is an unspoken mutual promise, it can, of course, be broken.

Such an abstract argument may become more persuasive if we turn from the subject of objectivity—the idealized spectators—to its object. We should expect the ritualization of the knower to be mirrored in the world he knows. Thus Gillispie writes of the nascent science of Galileo,

> . . . to look forward out of the Renaissance into Galileo's world was to stand alone peering into a nature deprived of sympathy and all humane association. That required both courage and power of abstract thought, which, one of the greatest of gifts, goes against the grain in all but the rarest temperaments. For sentiment rebels against the condition that nature sets the natural philosopher. This is that science communicate in the language of mathematics, the measure of quantity, in which no terms exist for good or bad, kind or cruel, and that she abandon our language of will and purpose and hope—abandon or denature or impoverish it, turning force, for example, from personal power into mass-times-acceleration.[6]

Nature sets conditions for the natural philosopher, however, only by means of natural philosophers' setting moral conditions for one another. Nature, like God, addresses mankind only through human spokesmen. A nature deprived of sympathy and all humane association is an object designed to be irrelevant to human differences of social rank, an object thus socially sanitized, about which scientists can safely be objective. A nature indifferent to their individual concerns will also be indifferent to their unavoidable concern with one another's concerns.

For by coming into one another's presence, scientists generate a host of ugly possibilities. They might assault one another, accuse one another of madness, denounce one another to the civil or ecclesiastical authorities. The nature the classical physicist investigates is ideally fitted to be the official focus of gatherings of inquirers who tacitly and unofficially reassure one another that they do not intend to do any of these things. Material particles possessed only of primary qualities offer no lures for feeling. The mathematical language in which scientists discuss them is altogether different from the language in which they conduct their everyday social commerce with one another. Thus the primary relationships that constitute the classical physicist as an affectionate human being exclude those very quantitative considerations essential to the primary qualities of his object. Subject and object of objectivity are precisely fitted to one another, and not by accident. Both are idealized projections, the one of a society of pure spectators, the other of a socially sanitized spectacle.

The growth of the dimensions of that spectacle, of its extent, of the number and kinds of experience incorporated in it, is the familiar story of the progress of the natural sciences since the Renaissance. Subject and object of objectivity have developed together, for to have an objective topic is the same as to know how to be objective about that topic. Here science has come so much to dominate our conception of nature that we find it difficult to recapture the prescientific experience of (what we have come to call) the natural world, intermixed as that experience was with elements we would today call miraculous, fabulous, or merely superstitious.[7] How readily and easily we distinguish those essentially verbal elements from what is natural and quantifiable testifies to how completely science has come to dominate our conception of nature and, concomitantly, our conception of ourselves as objective observers. For us today to see objectivity as problematical, we have to turn from the well-defined natural world to the observers' ritual work of defining one another. That social-scientific topic is among our concerns in the next section.

Society is an ideal of human togetherness, an historical individual, and a living collective subject. Since we encounter this ideal where we are—reasoning together—we decided to examine objectivity as a social process, in the hope of finding in that process some clue to the identity—as we put it, to the name—of the larger ideal that authorizes this particular form of community. We found that society authorizes the realization of the ideal of universal assent in the double form of the scientific disciplines, on the one hand, and the objective world they investigate, on the other. Although the scientific disciplines are particular groups composed of particular persons, it is fundamental to their organization that their membership may be indefinitely enlarged: the universality of the assent they strive to realize is the basis of their claims to prove. This universality-in-principle, this indifference to social differences, is concretely achieved through rules of propriety that guarantee safety in theoretical face-to-face situations by defining those situations as socially static, or, as we may say, socially sterile and sanitary, a relational asepsis aptly symbolized by the scientist's white lab coat.

§14 Sanitization and Typification

The human ability to put oneself in the other person's place, to take his point of view, to feel his feelings and understand his thoughts, appears only in historically conditioned forms. This mutuality or reciprocity of selfhood is the basis of morality; that is, it is at once the necessary condition and the imperative outcome of moral action. We referred to the activities that sustain the movement of reciprocity collectively as "the social process" or simply "society," individually as "social processes." We argued in the preceding section that objectivity can be construed as one such social process, that is, one way persons can reciprocally accredit one another as persons is by joining together in theoretical inquiry. Because objectivity was first established and developed in the natural sciences, we let this natural-scientific objectivity serve as our general case, postponing consideration of objectivity in the social sciences. We saw that the ceremonies through which nature is invoked and objectivity achieved in the natural sciences depend upon a prior joint development of the subject and object of objectivity, the former the scientific disciplines, the latter a mathematicized, socially sanitized spectacle, a nature interpreted not only as reliably predictable but also as indifferent to human differences of social rank.

The social sciences first arose as attempts to achieve over social affairs the same powers of prediction and control enjoyed by the natural sciences over nature. From this familiar, positivistic standpoint, the social sciences are branches of natural science, and social-scientific objectivity should therefore differ from objectivity in the better-established sciences only by society's being apparently more complex than most other natural systems. Men are gregarious animals whose natural habitat is society. Accordingly, as we pass from physics to biology to psychology to sociology, our explananda may grow progressively more complex, but what we mean by an "explanation" should remain in principle the same. In our own argument, when we said in §9 that love is the social reason for romantical decisions, we meant that laymen are required to explain those decisions by using coded discourse. We left open the possibility that the clear transcription of this code may be straightforwardly naturalistic and psychological; in other words, we left open the possibility of incorporating society and social relationships, love included, within the nature the natural scientist investigates.

On the other hand, the whole thrust of the functionalism of Part II was away from this implicit naturalism. We argued that love is not a feeling on a par with hunger or thirst, but the creation of an obligatory rhetoric, the referent of a noun in coded discourse. We pointed out that love is spoken of as a particularistic emotion, an emotion felt by one individual as such for another as such, where what counts as an "individual" is determined by culturally relative moral norms. Throughout Part II, we invoked society by contrasting nature with social convention, the natural conditions of collective action with collective action itself. This contrast is implied by the concept of socialization fundamental to functionalistic sociology. When we say there is an agency which trains us to curb our appetites and inhibit our natural drives, calling that agency "society" sets it over against the amorality of what merely happens, that is, contrasts it with nature. Thus the actions of the individual count as actions—sane, intelligible actions, "conduct" as opposed to "behavior"—only where they are thought to be regulated by moral rules, that is to say, only where society's collective action is seen to define them.

Our very concept of nature itself is socially determined. Where our ancestors found Satan and Original Sin opposing the benign influence of society, we find psychological forces. We not only affirm the natural scientist's concept of nature intellectually, we enforce it legally—through the institution of medicine, through regulations for safeguarding the public health, by licensing physicians, pharmacists, and other therapeutic specialists (and not licensing astrologers, palmists, and faith healers), and through our medical conception of insanity. Indeed—as we have seen—the natural sciences themselves are historically recent institutions, founded by Copernicus, Galileo, and their associates, and supported by an institutional rationale comparable to the rationales that support our political and religious institutions (which also make truth claims). The natural sciences owe their existence, then, fundamentally to society's enfranchisement of them and only derivatively to the nature they describe.

The world we invoke as "society" makes as plain and plausible a claim to explain nature as nature makes to explain it. Our strategy in this Part is to shift our attention from these dismayingly large, complex objects to the activities of inquiry of which they are the objective correlates. The functionalist assumes that society sustains itself by opposing nature. If this "nature" is the correlate of the natural scientist's objectivity, then objectivity in social science should differ essentially, should be more than merely an extension of the same explanatory principles to yet another class of natural objects. Explaining is a form of social intercourse, and we assume that here as elsewhere, the face-to-face form of the activity defines its indirect forms. Natural-scientific objectivity as a face-to-face social process is made possible by the sanitization of nature, the disengagement of nature from human desires, tastes, and interests and from the social relationships based on them. Since the social sciences are also theoretical inquiries, they must require an analogous disengagement or sanitization. But here the object to be sanitized is society itself. Directly or indirectly, the inquiring group inquires about what makes itself possible as a face-to-face group. There is an especially acute threat of unsanitary autoinvolvement, and it seems only reasonable to suppose that special means of sanitization must enable social scientists to cope with it.

Historically, topics have resisted scientific explanation for either or both of two kinds of reason. Some have been so complex and obscure that no one knew how to explain them, how to subsume them under accepted logical and mathematical explanatory principles. The overcoming of these resistances is the familiar staple of scientific progress, where once recalcitrant topics become "scientific" as logical and mathematical principles and experimental techniques are developed for explaining them. Some topics, on the other hand, have so intimately involved those social matters of which the scientific spectacle must be sanitized that trying to explain them threatened the objectivity of the explanation. Resistances of this second kind—unsanitary autoinvolvements—have by no means been confined to the social sciences. Astronomy, geology, and biology, for example, have had their famous periods of acute politicoreligious sensitivity. Necessarily, however, autoinvolvement in these natural-scientific disciplines must be less direct and less deep than it becomes in the social sciences, where the inquirer investigates not his habitat or appendages, but himself—his substance, rather than his attributes.

In order to determine what is special about the social sciences, we should look more closely at this quality of directness and depth in the objectivity that inquiry requires. What makes this depth possible, and what, if anything, limits it? Today, the natural scientist's concept of nature is securely institutionalized. Creationists, flat-earth theorists, and the like are no longer thought intellectually respectable, and our sensitivity to natural-scientific autoinvolvements has been largely overcome. The social scientist's concept of society seems less securely established and certainly far less clear. Nevertheless, the enormous growth of the social sciences would appear to be a peculiar and distinguishing characteristic of our own time and our own society.

It seems only reasonable to assume that the rise of social science points to an ideal. There are no corners of nature into which the natural scientist is unentitled to pry. Here we take the authority of the ideal of freedom of inquiry to be simply beyond question. Surely the same may be said of the social scientist. No part of society is safe from him; that is, the ideal of freedom of inquiry prevails there also. Our aim in this Part is to use the social process of inquiry as a clue to the identity of the larger social process which enfranchises it, that is, as a clue to the name of society itself. I shall assume that society confers upon the social scientist a freedom to inquire limited only by the logic of objectivity itself. This large assumption will govern the balance of the argument. If we can discover what the logical limits of objectivity are, this knowledge may enable us to determine how society acts through inquiry, and so to name society itself.

Assuming, then, that objectivity in social science is both possible and desirable, we want to know what makes it possible, how it is schematized, how it concretely comes about. In many social-scientific areas, we find employed devices familiar from their natural-scientific counterparts: quantification, the use of technical language, the institutionalization of "research" and of the researcher's role. Whatever else may be said in their favor, these are all essentially imitative ways of projecting a collective self-image of objectivity and sanitizing the subject-matter. Live and threatening autoinvolvements may be found even in such intrinsically quantified disciplines as economics and demography, but those obstacles to objectivity tend to be broad and political and therefore to be reflected only diffusely in face-to-face groups; hence they pose only the sorts of sanitization problem familiar from the natural sciences. In order to see the peculiarities of social-scientific objectivity, we should look first at the study of the human body, for the body is the point of contact between nature and society and is, of course, immediately problematic in face-to-face collaborative activity. The study of the body will point us toward topics where autoinvolvement is even deeper and more threatening, establishing a series. The end of this series will suggest what are the logical limits of objectivity.

Attitudes both cognitive and sentimental toward the body form a major part of the primary socialization required of persons as such. The body is the foundation of the individual's expressive activities, or—more accurately—that dimension of expressive activity in which he makes the morally fundamental claim about himself that he is an individual, unique, unduplicatable, inexhaustible by any set of predicates. We have seen that individuals claim and grant one another's selfhood or individuality reciprocally, this most fundamental ritual exchange being the precondition of all forms of social intercourse. In a given society—let it be our own—what might be called an ideology of the body will determine the most basic rules of face-to-face conduct, rules the violation of which exposes the offender to the accusation of madness. Thus individuals are required to present themselves to one another properly clothed, and to be denudative or to expose oneself is thought symptomatic of mental illness. The body's parts function differently in forming the primary bonds that define individuality, the genitals, for example, having a much greater bonding power than the elbows.

We have seen that theoretical situations are bounded by rules of relevance prescribing an official focus of attention and by rules of procedure prescribing how participants should behave—especially how they should act or refrain from acting upon one another, quarreling, forming friendships, ignoring one another, and so on. The same could be said of any face-to-face situation. Theoretical situations, however, constitute a limiting case, for in them social action is supposed to be completely suppressed, the situation thus being made safe for thought. Inquirers must thrust themselves as individuals entirely out of the official focus of attention and into the disattended background against which that official focus is figured. Whatever threatens this exclusion of persons, personalities, and personal relationships also threatens the objectivity defining the situation. Since in normal social intercourse, explicit mention of the ritually delicate parts of the body, especially the genital organs (the "private parts") is a bonding move, the body can be made the focus of theoretical attention only on condition that the everyday significance of attending to it is blocked.

The devices used to effect this blocking will be familiar: the wearing of special clothing, usually white; employment of a special vocabulary of Latin terms; a dignified, antiseptic setting where at least three persons are present; and so on. We say these are devices for "avoiding embarrassment," but surely the deeper point is that embarrassment is avoided by avoiding individuality. The official focus of attention is *typified*. In a crude and obvious sense, there is no such thing as "the penis"; there are many such organs, each attached to some individual. Each of these individuals has a private part explicit reference to which threatens what must be preserved if the distinction between objective inquiry and romantic solicitation (or destructive mockery) is to be preserved—namely, his privacy. The typical organ belongs to no one, and no one need glow with pride nor blush with shame over its typical properties. It can be talked about safely, therefore also objectively.

In the social sciences, sanitization depends upon typification. No such process is needed in natural science, for natural objects are not individual subjects. We may talk about them, but we do not talk to them, and they do not talk to one another about us. Those topics are socially threatening that tend to affect the individual directly as an individual. Under the normal circumstances of inquiry, topics of this sort must be kept in the officially disattended background. Such a topic may be brought into the official focus of attention, however, by being typified or understood as a universal, the common property of all, the private property of none. The figure is enriched, the ground correspondingly impoverished. One may see progress in the social sciences as, among other things, the gradual overcoming of these resistances that are due to socially threatening autoinvolvements. Now we want to know what limits the depth of this process of sanitization-by-typification, what limits the thoroughness and lack of reserve with which inquiry may turn inward upon itself and incorporate its own conditions.

Sexuality is a threatening topic because of the potency of sex as a bonding mechanism. Inquirers sanitize the topic by reciprocally assuring one another of the strength of their self-control and the correctness of their attitudes toward one another as potential sexual partners and rivals. Those sexual relationships, however, derive their significance from what they affirm about the primary bonds obtaining among the inquirers. Therefore when we turn from the expressive mechanism to what it is used to express, we move closer to the center of the individual. His deep-lying attitude toward bond formation, his sense of what it means to be a friend or lover or colleague, is his "personality," and that is at the inner core of him. Others will sense his sense of what primary bonds mean and be attracted or repelled accordingly. Explicitly defending a theory of bond formation is one way, and an effective way, of displaying what attracts or repels others. Hence in social psychology, where bond formation as such is studied, thought and action unavoidably merge, and we may well ask how objectivity is possible, how inquirers can possibly separate their soliciting of one another's favor from their study of what it means to solicit favor. The collaboration essential to the investigation seems to undercut its objectivity.

We have assumed that social science, including social psychology, is not only possible, but also desirable and morally worthy in itself, that is, without regard for any end beyond knowledge alone. A book on romantic love that did not make this assumption would be less than theoretical. When we study primary bonds, the ideals and values we study are our own. The society of inquirers dwells within the larger social world that enfranchises it. The inquirer is his own native informant. He understands the ideals of the society he inquires about because he himself responds to their prescriptive power. But his inquiry aims at proof, and in principle, a proof is capable of compelling universal assent, not just the assent of his specialist colleagues. In principle, therefore, society inquiring and society inquired about are the same: the corporate self-image the social psychologist affirms when he undertakes to prove incorporates just those individuals who define themselves by the primary bonds he inquires about.

The problem this autoinvolvement poses can be formulated in two ways. One can say either that the individual social psychologist must as it were disengage himself from himself, or alternatively, that the enfranchising group, society itself, must disengage itself from itself. The first formulation poses the problem of determining what special techniques, training, equipment, and institutional support systems make possible this apparently paradoxical sanitization-by-typification. The second formulation is logically prior, however, for, as we argued in §11, society itself is an individual whose activity of self-definition manifests itself in the particular individuals it creates. The disengagement that special techniques and devices make possible for the social psychologist depends upon society's prior definition of what constitutes an acceptable self. Hence before asking what techniques enable individual social psychologists to solve the problems of autoinvolvement peculiar to their discipline (a question we shall not pursue further), one ought first to take the point of view of society itself, that is, of our ideals themselves, and let the primary question be why they submit themselves to inquiry, why it should be part of their meaning that they allow themselves to become objects of theory—for here we ask about the cause of which the social psychologist's special techniques are only the result. The same fundamental ideals manifest themselves at once as the society of inquirers and the society inquired about. This is a distinctive feature of modern, Western society, for there alone do we find social science. It may well be that love and friendship among the Americans are rather like love and friendship among, say, the Hottentots; but there is the crucial difference that the Americans study and honor the study of themselves, while the Hottentots do not.

Sexuality and primary bonding are threatening topics because the individual is pressed to act with respect to them. Others expect him to act and grant him the freedom to do so. For example, he has the right to make his own friends and interpret in his own way the obligations and opportunities of friendship—on condition that he extend the same liberties to others. He exercises his sacred right to choose his own partners and policies in everything he does, even in joining sociological discussions of these choices, discussions where the topic must be sanitized by typification. When we turn to the sociology of religion, however, and to the sacred-profane distinction itself, we move behind these predicates of sexuality and personality to the subject that bears them. Others define the individual by the freedoms they grant him, just as they too are defined by the freedoms he grants them, but neither is free to withhold the freedoms of the other. One has, so to speak, a certain freedom of expression in the language of sociability, but the grammar of that language is collectively enforced and necessary.

In the sociology of religion—as we shall interpret that discipline here— we encounter the problem of objectivity in its most threatening form. Underneath what it permits in the way of individual variation, a society is held together by an implicit and pitilessly enforced agreement about what is meaningful and what meaningless, what real and what illusory. Recalling again Radcliffe-Brown's truism that "religion is the cement which holds society together," this agreement may be taken to be religious. Berger writes,

> Above all, society manifests itself by its coercive power. The final test of its objective reality is its capacity to impose itself upon the reluctance of individuals. . . . the fundamental coerciveness of society lies not in its machineries of social control, but in its power to constitute and to impose itself as reality.[8]

Individuals come together for objective inquiry in the sociology of religion on condition that they are members of the same society—our own—who recognize the same rites of sociability and requirements of socialization. Outside of the world of meanings defined by those rites and requirements lies meaningless anomy and madness. They come together through a common understanding of the legitimacy of their purpose. Society at large is the silent, approving witness of what they do, guaranteeing them that their actions at that time in those roles will not damage their ability to act at later times in other roles. The trust in one another that enables them to come together is founded upon their common understanding of what they propose to do, namely, to study the nature and function of religion in our society. In the sense in which this endorsement may be called "religious," it reaches the limit of autoinvolvement: the group comes together for an objective inquiry into the same endorsement that enables them to come together for this purpose. Objectivity about sexuality and primary bonding was accomplished by ignoring the individual as such and attending only to the type. Here, however, it is not the private individual, but that public individual, society itself, which must be ignored and typified. There is no Archimedean point outside society from which sociologists of religion could inquire into the efficacy and legitimacy of our religious beliefs, practices, and institutions, official and unofficial or "invisible."[9] Therefore their inquiry must be made possible by the self-typification of the individual they study. Objectivity must be our paramount ideal, the ultimate concern and basis of our invisible religion.

Such a conclusion is full of ambiguities, ambiguities we must resolve in the next section. In §8, we suggested that a Durkheimian, functional definition of religion is implied by the functionalistic method we were using then. We argued that the sociological distinction between primary and secondary relationships and the moral distinction between dignity and price parallel the religious distinction between the sacredness of persons and the profanity of other things. We said that one can use this distinction to define an unofficial, implicit, functional religion, an invisible religion that underlies the official sects and creeds of our secular society. Pursuing the argument in these terms would have enabled us to see romantic love as a religious phenomenon and "What is love?" as a religious question. Instead, we pursued the argument in socioeconomic and moral terms, making only occasional side-references to the religious parallels. Shifting to a religious vocabulary is obviously appropriate to our topic and in keeping with the ontological purpose we declared in the Introduction. But it will require clarification, for while religion has often been investigated as an objective phenomenon, objectivity has not often been investigated as a religious phenomenon.

§15 Ultimate Choice

We set out in the Introduction to give a philosophical theory of the question, "What is love?" We identified a "philosophical theory" as a theory of the question as a question, a theory that determines what the question asks and what sort of thing should count as an answer. We also said that one excellent test of such a theory of a question is the theory's ability to answer that question, and so we have examined a series of interpretations of "What is love?" together with the answers appropriate to each. In Part I, we examined the layman's conception of love as a mysterious, unanalyzable feeling and the layman's interpretation of "What is love?" as the question "Which feeling is it?" Then we examined—admittedly, in no very great detail—the psychologist's conception of love as an unmysterious natural phenomenon and the psychologist's interpretation of "What is love?" as the question "Which natural phenomenon is it?" In Part II, we turned to the sociologist's conception of romantic love as a social institution and the sociologist's interpretation of "What is love?" as the question "What is the social function of that institution?"

All three interpretations turn "What is love?" into a question about where a certain object—a feeling, a drive, an institution—is located within an all-inclusive whole, a world. We found we had invoked two such worlds or ultimate objects, nature and society. In §11, we argued that the second of these, society, might better be looked upon as not primarily an object, but rather as a knowing and acting collective subject. We surmised that love might be another name for that subject. Hence in the present Part III, we have undertaken to determine what or who society is, that is, to determine society's proper name.

This unusual formulation has several advantages. If indeed, as §11 argues, society is an individual, then that individual as denoted by its proper name is ontologically prior to that individual under any mere description. Moreover, society first entered the argument not as one of the topics inquired about but as a fundamental condition of our activity of inquiry— namely, when we used "society" to invoke the tradition of objective inquiry in social science. We inquired, as one might say, "in the name of" that tradition and the ideal of objectivity that defines it. Participants in any joint enterprise are entitled to call upon one another in the name of the guiding ideal of that enterprise, for each is presumed to have committed himself to that ideal, or, said differently, to have committed himself to the others through that ideal. Calling upon someone (at least implicitly, by *his* proper name) in the name of the ideal reminds him of what he owes to it, or, through it, to the others. Proper names used in this invocative way are often qualified by "sacred." The name's sacredness manifests itself in the sacred commitments or primary relationships contracted through it. Note that while these idioms are found most often in religious and political ceremonies, the social dynamics they articulate are as common as organized activity itself. We saw, however, that the commitment we acknowledge with the sacred name of social science is not ultimate, for it is made possible by our own society's unique cherishing of this form of theoretical inquiry. The name we finally call upon—could we but name it—is our own, the name of our highest ideal, our collective sacred self. Asking for society's proper name, then, points up not only the ontological priority of the problem, but also its religious intimacy.

In §4.2, we argued that explicit communication presupposes tacit, identity-establishing communication. We reason together explicitly on the basis of an implicit agreement about the legitimacy of reasoning and of ourselves as reasoners, an agreement that society enfranchises and that we must continually renegotiate and reconstitute. In §13 we examined the particular form this reciprocity or continual generating of implicit agreement takes in the natural sciences, and in §14 we examined its social-scientific form. We found that the former depends on what we called the "sanitization" of threatening social autoinvolvements, and we found that in the latter this sanitization depends upon a process of typification. We asked next where typification might be found in its most extreme and characteristic form, and we found this in the sociology of religion, where the ultimate agreement that is the enfranchising society itself becomes typified. If indeed, as Durkheim asserts, society itself is what is ultimately sacred, then the sociology of religion's right and power to profane that sacred mystery by explaining it seems to require an explanation. Here we argued that it must be the case that the explanandum provides its own explanation, that we as a society regard explanation as our most sacred rite.

The definition of "religion" is a topic of long-standing philosophical dispute.[10] To name only a single alternative, religion may be defined either substantively or functionally, either in terms of what it is or in terms of what it does. Tillich's well-known definition may be taken to epitomize the substantive alternative:

> Religion is the state of being grasped by an ultimate concern, a concern which qualifies all other concerns as preliminary and which itself contains the answer to the question of the meaning of our life.[11]

Substantively, we think of a religion as a set of beliefs about such ultimate, supernatural topics as the existence of God and the meaning of life. A body of rituals and a communion of believers will be organized around those beliefs, but the beliefs themselves are thought to be the operative element, and their efficacy is supposed to depend on their truth. In our society, such beliefs are held to be a private matter, an option of the individual, who may accept one set or another or perhaps none at all—for many compete for his allegiance. If one asks what properties a set of beliefs must have to qualify as "religious" in this conventional, substantive sense, perhaps no more than a loose historical answer is possible. We are prone to fall back upon "ultimate" and "supernatural," terms that in this usage seem to mean little more than "unprovable." As a collection of proofs, a science can in principle compel universal assent; but a religion cannot, for we will not let one do so. There may or may not be a God—the individual is entitled to decide as he pleases. But there *are* contagious diseases, and quarantine laws are enforced by the authorities.

Compelle intrare.[12] Historically, religious beliefs have been enforced and the powers of government have rested on a religious sanction. How can a concern that cannot be enforced be genuinely "ultimate"? Let us suppose that I have an ultimate concern for the meaning of life. That does not entitle me to interpret "the meaning of life" in such a manner as would justify my taking your life, nor even my taking my own. We require private "ultimate" concerns to be kept private, kept out of the common public world where they might lead to genuinely ultimate conflicts. Surely, by definition, the individual has an ultimate concern for whatever defines him as an individual. We define him as an individual (one may add, tautologically but informatively, as a sane individual) by allowing him to choose, among other things, his own religion—on condition, of course, that he extend the same freedom to others. From a functionalistic point of view, then, behind our many official, substantively defined religions, there must be a concept of the sacred that performs for us the same function performed for our ancestors by the Church Universal, the function of creating us by requiring us to define one another as sacred beings whose powers are formidable and whose rights must be respected. What we take to be sacred is the private individual and the primary relationships that define him, relationships centered in the family.

What we take to be ultimately sacred, however, is not the private individual as such, but all of us, the social process that creates private individuals. In order to ask what this process—society—is, we asked what is the science of society. We asked that question in a pointed form by asking what makes objectivity in the social sciences possible, and we asked that question in turn in a pointed form by asking what makes objectivity in the sociology of religion possible. We worked up to this question gradually, first by examining the sanitization of threatening autoinvolvements in the study of sexuality, then by examining it in the study of primary bonding. We came away with the clue that, in both cases, the threatening topic is sanitized by being typified. And we have the additional clue that typification is not so to speak an extramundane gimmick, but an activity sanctioned by the very ideals the social scientist studies.

Now apply these two clues to religion. We have seen that objectivity in those face-to-face inquiries that ground the sciences depends upon the discussants implicitly agreeing to set aside action in favor of thought by holding their own social relationships constant during the course of the inquiry. They are to think together rather than to act upon one another. This holding in abeyance of defensive action depends upon their sense of safety in one another's presence. This sense of safety in turn depends upon an implied mutual concession of good character. In particular, they concede one another's capacities for self-restraint in those matters where the individual is thought pressed to act. Thus he will have—or, more to the point, will be presumed to have—sexual drives that he must inhibit and a need for companionship and social approval that he must restrain. Therefore these restraints and inhibitions are threateningly autoinvolved topics that can be inquired about only after being sanitized by typification. We may undertake an objective, theoretical inquiry into the typical individual's need for friendship. If our topic were your very own loneliness, however, then the inquiry might be therapeutical, but it could not be objective and theoretical. We think "Religion is a private affair" a truism and our laws make membership in religious organizations entirely optional. Viewed in historical and anthropological perspective, however, an ultimate concern for the meaning of human life in general and one's own life in particular is the least private and optional of concerns, and the drive for religious communion is far stronger than the drives for sexual gratification or social approval, for these latter drives are merely specializations of it. Therefore if, in the sociology of religion, this altogether urgent and paramount drive for religious communion is sanitized by being typified, we may well ask how this is possible, how individuals can possibly agree among themselves to set aside their most fundamental drive to seek agreement.

We know that in principle—and our topic is our ideals or principles—society inquiring and society inquired about are the same. No part of society is safe from sociology, and there is no Archimedean point outside the social world from which the inquirer might obtain a perspective uninfluenced by the society that legitimates his own activity of inquiry. Therefore our second clue to the possibility of objective inquiry about our fundamental ideals is that this possibility must be built into those ideals: typifiability must be essential to them. Therefore when we ask how sociologists of religion can sanitize the religious drive by typifying it, in one sense the answer is easy and a contemporary commonplace. They can because they must, because society has long since secularized itself, separated church and state, forbidden the individual to impose his religious beliefs (now thought private) upon others—an historical accomplishment in which we take no little pride.

In another sense, however, this sanitization of the religious drive seems more puzzling. Objective inquiry as a social process depends upon the inquirers' sense of safety in one another's presence. The theoretical ideal schematizes itself through that sense of safety and its elaborate support system of laws, institutions, and customs. What was once safety in the fellowship of the religious communion has become safety from the social controls that sustained that communion, from excommunications, inquisitions, and accusations of heresy. Reflecting on Tillich's definition of religion, one may argue that since this secular freedom is demonstrably, indeed, legally more ultimate than the individual's ultimate or religious concern, by that very fact it is entitled to be called "religious," even though its religiosity is (as Luckmann puts it) "invisible." On the other hand, pluralistic, secular civil society and the scientific disciplines that flourish by its license seem ill-equipped to replace the warmth and comfort of the religious communion, with its vivid pictures of life, death, and transcendence. Although in some ways science does resemble a religion, still theory is not practice and restraining the religious impulse is not the same as indulging it. How can a negative activity that supplies none of the substantive content and practical guidance of a religion nevertheless perform the function of one?

Here we must bear in mind the level of abstraction on which the argument endeavors to move. Our aim is to understand society's self-definition, not to determine how particular institutions and practices should be labeled. We deal with our fundamental ontological commitment, our invocation of the world. The world is not something one might explain, but the self-defining action of an ideal of explanation. As we undertook to explain romantic love, we found ourselves invoking two such worlds, nature and society, each claiming to encompass the other. We asked how such a conflict might be reconciled, and we found that social-scientific objectivity both encompasses and extends objectivity in the natural sciences. Here we found our highest ideal of objectivity, an objectivity whose legitimation we took to be peculiarly characteristic of our own society.

Historically, religion has offered a third such world, a sacred canopy (in Berger's phrase) extending over whatever is, giving each person and thing a time, place, and significance. Today, however, religious explanations are without authority. Authorities exist to correct the individual who refuses to acknowledge that tuberculosis is contagious or that grand-jury deliberations are secret. By contrast, religious beliefs are optional and differences in belief are tolerated. Something no one has to listen to may be a comfort or a curiosity, but not a proof. The argument is not that might makes right, but that the best way to discover what we really think true is to look for what we really confer power upon. A highest ideal may manifest itself subjectively through a sense of seriousness, but it manifests itself objectively and demonstratively through a system of social controls. That thought, of course, underlies functionalism.

Proof is the opposite of mystery. The sacred mysteries of religion are no longer publicly enforceable, but their impotence has a positive significance. They re-emerge as the property and right of the private individual, who may cherish them in his inwardness and celebrate his own sacredness by shielding them from others. Surely the process that produces so potent a deity as the private individual may itself make a reasonable claim, if not to divinity, at least to whatever functions as divinity's contemporary descendant.

The sociology of religion, in which individuals come together to inquire about one another's most cherished and fundamental beliefs, is the highest celebration of sociological objectivity. This objectivity is possible because those beliefs are typified, treated as impersonal objects, scrupulously separated from the inner, private persons who cherish them. Typification is built into those beliefs themselves, for while the individual may think he imparts his deepest confidence to his gods, he imparts in fact a far deeper confidence to his fellow inquirers, whom he trusts to regard his private inwardness as the most sacred of mysteries. Beyond and above them, he lays his trust upon the ideal of theoretical inquiry and the society that supports it through the democratic political system with its tradition of due process, its freedoms of speech, press, and religion, and its deep commitment to secular education. This ideal and this society are the collective ultimate choice in which the individual participates and by virtue of which he exists as a private person. The sacred canopy under which he shelters seems to stop at his skin, leaving him alone within in godlike seclusion.

But that seclusion is only a religious artifact, a creature of ceremony. The mutual trust that enables individuals to come together is the precondition of overt theoretical inquiry, but it is also the product of unceasing covert communication, of a constant flow of mutual reassurances whose efficacy depends on not being noticed. The extent and intimacy of the topics inquirers can safely reason together about testifies to their respect for one another's privacy, but even more to their utter transparency to one another, for the latter makes the former possible. Each understands the countless ways in which the others have promised not to take advantage of him. The language of that mutual reassurance, the capacity to say that we can share time and space and can engage in inquiry in spite of differences in social identity, in age, sex, class, race, religion, citizenship, and so on, has taken up and articulated all the elaborate institutional apparatus undergirding the discussion, for the inquirer's absolute freedom of private thought rests on an equally absolute satisfaction of the necessities of public action. This language of universal assent is an historical achievement of the very first rank, and a fragile achievement. Thus such a public emergency as a war tends to convert privacy from an automatic privilege into a dangerous luxury, and in those nations that regard themselves as perpetually at war, such a reflective accomplishment as the sociology of religion is unknown.

As we noted in §13, historically the natural sciences, especially physics, have provided the baseline of objectivity, the simplest, clearest experiences and principles that establish the meaning of the term. In mathematical physics, the theoretical ideal of pure spectators confronting a socially sanitized spectacle, disinterested observers recording the features of a world that reciprocates their disinterest, is most obviously realized. That objectivity is achieved by means of a technical, mathematical language altogether different from the ordinary language in which physicists conduct their social affairs. Under the influence of Wittgenstein and the symbolic-logic movement, the Logical Positivists of the earlier decades of this century tried to construct an "ideal scientific language," an artificial substitute for ordinary language that would bring to the more general and qualitative areas of inquiry the impersonality and precision found in physics. We would call such a language "ideally sanitized."

Wittgenstein himself subsequently repudiated the Logical Positivist's program. He argued that ordinary language is inescapable—inescapable because an artificial language cannot be constructed except by defining it within ordinary language. Therefore sanitization is something that can be accomplished in ordinary language, and in a fundamental sense can be accomplished there only. We have taken the contemporary flourishing of the social sciences to be a confirmation of this thesis. Thus in our own day the ideal of theoretical objectivity first clearly defined in seventeenth-century physics has extended itself to what would appear to be a logical limit, the sociology of religion, in which society becomes an object to itself, in which the social process that lives by generating our most fundamental sentiments legitimates the unsentimental analysis of that very process itself. Our society is only one of many, our religions, visible and invisible, merely typical efforts to create meaning and community in the face of human recalcitrance and a hostile nature. Here that ideal figure, the pure spectator, is purged of all his loyalties except his loyalty to theory itself. He appears to stand on a dizzying pinnacle of objectivity, an Archimedean point quite outside the world and outside of himself too. Thus Berger writes in the preface to *The Sacred Canopy*,

> While at certain points the argument moves on levels of considerable abstraction, it never leaves (at least not intentionally) the frame of reference of the empirical discipline of sociology. Consequently it must rigidly bracket throughout any questions of the ultimate truth or illusion of religious propositions about the world.[13]

134

III. Inquiry and the Inquirer

The empirical discipline of sociology describes a society it never made; otherwise it would not be empirical. We have suggested, however, that this conception of social-scientific inquiry presupposes that the society it inquires into (most intimately in the sociology of religion) has the peculiar and distinguishing characteristic of extending just this franchise to inquiry. Inquiry is the enactment of the ideal of universal assent: in principle, the community of inquirers may become coextensive with the society about which it inquires. It is as if the ideal of universal assent created for itself a world of individuals by giving itself a religious significance. If this is our ultimate ideal, then it is an ultimate collective choice. We can name it or point to it, but we cannot justify it, for it is its own justification.

This ideal is an ideal of community, of human solidarity. Therefore as any such ideal must, it prescribes positive primary relationships, the reciprocity of putting oneself in the other person's place, seeing in him the same sacred individuality one must see in oneself. Love in this generic sense is always a name for society and the tie that binds is always blest. We can ask further, however, how the ideal of universal assent schematizes itself through our particular system of primary relationships, a system dominated, as we have seen, by the romantical code. Since a system of primary relationships is a definition of individuality, we can ask what conception of the individual is appropriate to a society of inquirers and how the romantical code contributes to that conception.

We know that inquiry presupposes inquirers, who cooperate in the projection of a disciplinary self-image of objectivity, an image in which each of them is individually portrayed as a free intellect, a source of unbiased judgments. Kant's argument for freedom of the will in the *Foundations of the Metaphysics of Morals* is well known:

> Now we cannot conceive of a reason which consciously responds to a bidding from the outside with respect to its judgments, for then the subject would attribute the determination of its power of judgment not to reason but to an impulse.[14]

By definition, the inquirer must think himself free to decide on the basis of the evidence, regardless of his personal reaction to it, that is, regardless of how he may feel about it. Our strategy in §13 was to concentrate not on this obligatory inner state, but on how those social situations in which the individual is obliged to display this inner state to others are organized. Thus whether or not anyone ever has actually possessed this freedom of will and purity of motivation, it is a public fact that inquirers are required to credit one another with it: here the outward images of inner states are manifest objects of social controls. Those controls regulate the constant flow of overt and covert communications in which inquirers cooperate in maintaining a group self-image of objectivity. The controls therefore depend upon a rhetoric, a language of universal assent that permits inquirers to communicate their objectivity to one another. In §13 and §14, we saw how that language of universal assent has emerged from the specialized confines of mathematical physics and has come to include ordinary language itself.

We have learned how to accredit one another's objectivity even while inquiring about the most intimate topics, and in the very language of intimacy itself, ordinary language. To credit someone with objectivity, however, means to make him personally inexplicable. One may explain why some bias corrupts his judgment, but not why he is free from bias, for if he chooses to be objective, by definition this must be a free and inexplicable choice. When one says that he is objective, one credits him with that control over his feelings which objectivity requires. If, however, his free judgment is said to be inexplicable, then by the same token the personal feelings which do not corrupt that judgment are said to be inexplicable too, for those controlled feelings are simply the reverse side of that judgment. We saw in §14 that feelings may become objects of inquiry only as typified, for as personal they are not different from the necessarily mysterious and sacred individual who feels them; hence they too must be mysterious and sacred. The point is a point of rhetoric: we make the distinction, crucial to inquiry, between explaining someone and explaining to him by portraying him as personally inexplicable. The rhetoric of feeling must support this portrayal. It must enable inquirers to declare their respect for one another by declaring their respect for one another's feelings, feelings that are respected by being placed beyond the reach of explanation.

In the Introduction, we proposed two criteria for concluding our argument. We said that our theory of love and of the question "What is love?" must be an ontological theory, a theory that evaluates the reality of love in comparison to the reality of other things. Such a demand seemed impossible to fulfil, and that apparent impossibility provided our second criterion: we said our theory must explain why we, as laymen, initially thought such a theory impossible. We see now that we thought a theory of love impossible because our society's very dedication to theory itself seems to make such a theory impossible. Those personal feelings of which romantic love is the chief and cynosure function rhetorically as pretheoretical conditions of theory. Objectivity as a social process is made possible by granting the individual a private, inner being that escapes typification by being literally unspeakable. In spite of this literal unspeakability, however, personal feelings must of course be expressed and the individual must be provided with a language for expressing them, a language in which primary relationships can be negotiated. Society provides him therefore with a metaphorical language, a code, an idiom in which he can at once betray his secrets and preserve their secrecy, at once open his mind and conceal its contents. We have seen the place of the romantical code in this counterexplanatory metaphorical language.

Scientific time, the time of predictions, is well-defined time, the time we familiarly define as "the independent variable of the science of mechanics." A society organized around the ideal of universal assent must project itself, so it seems, onto that well-defined time, locating within it even such a pretheoretical condition of theory as the individual and the free choices and personal feelings said to constitute his individuality. As we have seen, society enforces the natural scientist's conception of nature, a nature assumed entirely explainable, a nature in which every event is assumed to follow from preceding events in accordance with a law. We draw our models of explanation from the natural sciences, where to explain an event means to show how it had to occur when and where it did: the language of universal assent is deterministic. In the personal affairs that we exclude from objective inquiry, however, we also explain our actions, providing one another with accounts, apologies, excuses, justifications, and pretexts. In spite of the diversity of their forms and functions, one may suggest that these explanations ultimately derive their ritual plausibility from their metaphorical mimicry of objective explanation. We represent ourselves, thus, as determined by just such false forces and sham compulsions as the romantical code provides. Those metaphorical forces and compulsions conceal what are in fact free choices, for that is what we implicitly call them when we turn to the serious business of inquiry.

Clearly the conditions of inquiry are more real than the objects of inquiry, for the latter depend on the former. Therefore the most real thing of all must be our collective choice of a way of life. The next most real must be the individuals who live that life, for if they collectively are the choosers, they individually are what the choice is all about. They live their lives by making free choices, some of which they conceal—even from themselves— behind a facade of rhetoric. Where romantic love is concerned, we have seen that that rhetoric has its legitimate purposes. Objective explanation is not among those purposes, but that does not detract from their legitimacy.

Here, then, we have satisfied the two criteria proposed in the Introduction for concluding our theory of love and "What is love?" We have shown what love really is, and we have shown why at first we thought it impossible to show what love really is. This task being completed, we must now turn to the more general task we set ourselves in the Introduction. There we said that we did not choose the questionable question "What is love?" for its own sake, but as an example. We chose it in order to give an exposition and defense of a set of philosophical principles, on the principle that the proof of a theory of proof lies in the proving. Having shown our principles at work, our final task must be to state them explicitly. That is the topic of the next and concluding section.

§16 Skepticism

The reader who has had the patience and curiosity to follow a lengthy abstract argument has the right to ask the author where the argument fits into the world, why he wrote it, and what he hopes it will accomplish. These are questions usually answered in a preface. There the author tells how he thinks the reading public is ignorant and how he proposes to relieve its ignorance. The second "how" is the how of method. In the beginning of this book, on the other hand, philosophy was identified as the science of questions, that discipline which determines what are the different kinds of question and what methods will decide them. So defined, philosophy is the study of method. One might well ask what is the method of the study of method; the answer to that rather questionable question belongs at the end of such a study, not at the beginning.

"Method" carries with it certain conventional expectations. The method for studying something is supposed to be different from the study of that something, that is, a method is supposed to be applied. There are two ingredients in a science, a method and a subject matter, and the actual study of the subject matter is the application of the method to it. In the Introduction, we said that questionable questions are the proper subject matter of philosophy, questions whose large importance we sense but whose methodological reference is unclear to us. We said that the philosopher's task is to theorize about these questions for the purpose of transforming them into something more fruitful and manageable. In this book, we have undertaken such a transformation of "What is love?" From a conventional point of view, then, the book ought to end by endorsing a philosophical method, a general prescription for the study of questionable questions, some stepwise procedure for transforming them from bad actors to good.

The idea of a "questionable question," however, seems not to fit these conventional expectations. Questionable questions refuse to fit the explanatory slots we have available for them. They baffle us because they upset the conventional understandings we share when we unite in that most social of activities, explanation. Sometimes, as we have seen with "What is love?", they threaten to raise precisely those personal issues that impersonal, objective inquiry must exclude. The conventional understandings that underlie inquiry constitute the definite world, the world we agree upon, our present; therefore what lies outside them has to be—for us and for the present—ill defined. Hence a list of questionable questions would be however long one wished to make it, and a general method for transforming them would be what is least appropriate of all, another convention.

Nevertheless, philosophy is a definite discipline and a definite activity, and to write a definite philosophy book means to make a recommendation for the future of the discipline. Although contemporary philosophy has many branches, I have assumed that ontology is the final cause of the discipline, so that to show the philosophical significance of a questionable question means to show its ontological significance. Among contemporary ontological traditions, I have tried to address myself primarily to the skeptical, empiricist, "analytic" tradition, for that is the center around which Anglo-American philosophy turns. The modern skeptical tradition begins with Descartes' systematic doubt, a beginning that also gives it its hardest problem, which is how doubt can be systematic. The idea of a "method for being skeptical" is a confusing idea. I want to conclude this philosophical essay by examining that idea and its significance.

The ancient philosophical skeptic tried to refute proofs for the existence of any entity transcending immediate experience. So far in this book, we have used "skepticism" simply to refer to the requirement that existence claims be proved. "Proof," of course, has several meanings, hence before a claim can be proved to us, we must agree with the claimer about what sort of thing shall count as proof. That problem implies the problem of the modern philosophical skeptic. In our theory of love, we distinguished two general types of factual proof, two ways of proving existence claims, the natural-scientific and the social-scientific. We saw that proofs of either type entail fundamental ontological commitments to the existence either of nature or of society. Nature and society themselves enter inquiry through methodological assumptions: we assume that they exist in general in order to construct proofs about how they exist in detail. The modern philosophical skeptic questions whether these methodological assumptions themselves can be proved. Descartes and Hume asked this only of natural science, but we must ask it of social science as well.

Whether methodological assumptions themselves can be proved or—to use a softer word, "justified"—is an obscure question that surely itself needs a justification. Throughout Part III, we have emphasized that proving is a social activity, a form of communication, therefore a group accomplishment. Society enfranchises theoretical groups, the scientific and scholarly disciplines, whose special function is to prove. Society might be said to deed over to each of these groups authority over a certain class of questions—the authority, namely, to decide who counts as a prover and what counts as a proof where those questions are concerned. We may ask, then, whom one might ask for a proof or for justification of a discipline's method of proof. It seems inappropriate to ask this of the members of the discipline themselves, for what counts as proof to them, at least in their capacity as experts, is a question internal to the discipline. And certainly one cannot ask this of the public at large, for they have deeded over the authority of expertness to the discipline.

To be sure, the intellectual authority a discipline receives from the public is limited to a particular class of questions: chemists are expert on chemical questions, biologists on biological questions. There is also a boundary between chemistry and biology, a boundary now given over to biochemistry. The boundary a discipline draws between itself and a neighbor belongs as much to the neighbor as to itself. When we say that these disciplinary boundaries are often conventional, as indeed they often are, we mean that the disciplines as it were agree among themselves where the one's authority is to stop, the other's to begin. This image of interdisciplinary agreement may seem to idealize the squabbling world of science and scholarship, but that is the point of it, to point to a feature of the ideal of proof. The fact that there are boundary conventions implies that the intellectual authority of a discipline is absolute. No outside agency is entitled to limit it, whether that agency be another discipline, a government, a church, or anything else. Indeed, disciplines arise historically—out of philosophy—through the growth of public acceptance of separate disciplinary authority over particular classes of questions, an authority entitling groups of experts not to defer their judgments about those questions to anyone save one another.

"Time was," Kant writes, "when metaphysics was entitled the Queen of all the sciences."[15] Philosophy—whose center and final cause is metaphysics or ontology—is the matrix from which they all arose. Of course this maternal imagery implies that the child establishes its own independent authority and need no longer defer to the parent. So physics is no longer called "natural philosophy," and the other special sciences have also gone their separate ways. Just as the medieval Papacy became merely another warring temporal power, philosophy today has become merely another separate discipline exercising its own limited authority. However, if we ask "Authority over exactly what?" then we raise a question that has baffled twentieth-century philosophers—rather notoriously, in fact.

Is there a class of peculiarly philosophical questions, questions about which the philosopher might call himself an "expert," over which he might exercise an expert's authority? We have said that philosophy studies questionable questions, but questions are in our sense "questionable" because we cannot tell who ought to be given authority over them. We may dismiss immediately the implied suggestion that the philosopher should serve as a sort of interdisciplinary referee. Who would listen to him? Like grown children, the other disciplines settle their disputed questions among themselves, neither wanting nor needing philosophical interference. Indeed, contemporary Anglo-American empiricism turned to the precise, "analytical" treatment of detached questions out of skeptical disbelief in the authority of the nineteenth century's grand, synthetical systems. But which questions ought to be detached, and how ought they to be detached, and what ought they to be detached from? The old program of system building had the virtue of dealing explicitly with the question of where philosophy belongs in the whole intellectual enterprise. That question is still pertinent.

When we ask what the philosopher is expert about, we invoke a concept in ordinary use, the concept of the theoretical expert, the technical specialist. Proof is a social process: the expert draws his authority from his discipline; the discipline in turn draws its authority from the public. Experts in a discipline decide among themselves who they are, but that there are experts about a certain subject—that is decided by public consensus. The expert is presumed to have had special experiences that laymen have not had: he has conducted experiments or surveys, examined original works and documents, or acquired clinical experience. Existence proofs are the real index of his authority. When the economists prove that there are recessions or the biologists that there are viruses, then those things exist, and the public modifies its view of the world accordingly. Real money is spent and real power redistributed.

Measured by this standard, contemporary philosophy is without authority. There are no philosophical experts, just as no doubt there never has been a Platonic philosopher-king. Like the mathematician, the philosopher is trained in reasoning. However, while mathematicians might well lay claim to the special experience of reasoning about an essentially esoteric subject-matter, such a claim from a philosopher seems inappropriate. Philosophers reason about other people's reasoning. In this general sense of "logic," they are logicians. But authority over someone else's reasoning always resides in that other person himself. He is the ultimate judge of his own reasoning: that is what it means to credit him with the ability to reason. The logician appeals to his judgment, draws upon his authority. To say, then, that philosophers are experts on logical questions is tantamount to admitting that they are not "experts" in the ordinary sense at all—and surely the ordinary sense is the only sense that matters.

"Logic," of course, has a narrower or stricter sense in which it names a specialty that has flourished in this century. As logic has flourished, however, it has also gradually withdrawn from philosophy, becoming a separate mathematical discipline with its own organization, its own experts, and its own independent authority. The concomitant rise of a "philosophy of logic" parallel to the philosophies of science, art, and the like suggests that when reasoning about a class of questions becomes a definite activity dealing with definite objects by definite rules, then philosophers begin to feel that they can no longer rightly claim that class of questions as their own. Thus logical questions have become "technical"—an adjective inapplicable in principle to the study of method. However, if philosophers can no longer speak authoritatively about logical necessity, one may well ask what in the world is left for them to be expert about.

My answer is that the conventional concept of the expert or technical specialist does not apply to philosophy, and indeed never has applied to it. Proofs and explanations are forms of communication. Like all forms of communication, formal proofs in the special sciences depend on informal conditions, on the process of tacit coming-to-agreement we have examined in Part III. This process generates well-defined reasoners with well-defined questions to settle. It is the ground against which reasoning figures. We embrace the theoretical ideal, we say that a proof can compel assent, but to say this in any definite way, we must have agreed what shall count as genuine assent and what as bias and interest. There are no experts about this process in which the theoretically relevant separates itself from the practically irrelevant, for the process itself produces both bodies of experts and the well-defined questions they are expert about. They are its result. A definite, defensible account of the process simply creates another result, another subject-matter we know how to reason about.

For this reason, philosophical interest has traditionally centered upon questionable questions, questions that seem to sprout between the cracks of science, art, history, and politics and to resist settlement because they somehow question what we call "settling a question." These necessarily ill-defined questions enable philosophy to represent the theoretical ideal as such, before its differentiation into separate specialties. They give us a sidewise glimpse at the movement of vague intellectual discomforts into demonstrable facts and certified demonstrators, allowing us perhaps to help the movement along a little. So conceived, philosophical proofs—and I have tried to give one—should not be said to "compel" assent, as if intellectual assent, of all things, could be compelled. Political metaphors, images of persuasion and leadership, seem more appropriate. Nor should a philosopher have a "position," as if the movement of inquiry stopped somewhere. Instead he should have a movement from questionable questions to questions less questionable.

The theoretical ideal, which lives in the movement of inquiry, assuredly exists and is real: there our ontology comes to rest. But ours is a skeptical discipline. Often we try to show others how their explanations push their principles beyond their proper limits, there encountering tautology, dogmatism, edification, and partisanship. We have spoken of these as pathologies of explanation, but that is to stress only the negative side of them, for explanation is a social activity. As a rule, we encounter tautology concealed within ritual, dogmatism in the sharing of beliefs, edification in the promotion of common ideals, and partisanship in the sense of collective loyalty. These are the mediums through which organizations organize themselves. We argued in §13 that the real agent of proof in the special sciences is not the individual scientist, but the collective self-image of objectivity projected by the discipline. The philosophical analogue seems problematic, for a "collective self-image of skepticism" is a banner ideally maladapted for rallying around. So we are endlessly contentious, and we should become suspicious when we cease to be so. When we find ourselves disputing well-defined questions, organizing ourselves into bodies of "experts," making philosophy "technical," then we should become skeptical about our own skepticism. And then we should seek out different, more genuinely questionable questions to be skeptical about. That is the reason for this book on "What is love?"

Notes

INTRODUCTION: *CONSTRUCTING A THEORY* (pages 1–6)

1. My use of masculine and feminine names and pronouns is dictated entirely by stylistic convenience.
2. Adapted from Calvin S. Hall, *A Primer of Freudian Psychology* (New York. New American Library, 1954), p. 82.

PART I. *THE CONCEPT OF LOVE* (pages 7–35)

1. Ludwig Wittgenstein, *Philosophical Investigations*, tr. G. E. M. Anscombe (New York: The Macmillan Co., 1953), Part I, Par. 11.
2. See Morton M. Hunt, *The Natural History of Love* (Scranton, Pa.: Minerva Press, 1959), especially Chapter V.
3. For "civil inattention," see Erving Goffman, *Behavior in Public Places: Notes on the Social Organization of Gatherings* (New York: The Free Press of Glencoe, 1963), pp. 84–88.
4. Charles Horton Cooley, *Social Organization* (New York: Charles Scribner's Sons, 1909), pp. 23 ff. (New York: Schocken Books, 1962), pp. 23 ff.
5. See, for example, Immanuel Kant, *Critique of Practical Reason and Other Writings in Moral Philosophy*, tr. L. W. Beck (Chicago: University of Chicago Press, 1949), p. 92.
6. See Kant, *Religion within the Limits of Reason Alone*, tr. T. M. Greene and Hoyt Hudson (New York: Harper and Bros., 1960), p. 34.
7. Erving Goffman, *Interaction Ritual: Essays on Face-to-Face Behavior* (Garden City, N.Y.: Anchor Books, 1967), p. 47.
8. See Erving Goffman, *Asylums: Essays on the Social Situation of Mental Patients and Other Inmates* (Garden City, N.Y.: Anchor Books, 1961), pp. 150–151.
9. Goffman, *Behavior in Public Places*, p. 17.
10. See Erving Goffman, *The Presentation of Self in Everyday Life* (New York: Doubleday and Co., 1959), pp. 2–4.
11. See, for example, H. D. F. Kitto, *The Greeks* (Baltimore: Penguin Books, 1951), p. 94.
12. Goffman, *Interaction Ritual*, pp. 92–95.
13. *Interaction Ritual*, pp. 47–95.
14. See the discussion of "decompensation" in James C. Coleman, *Abnormal*

Psychology and Modern Life (Chicago: Scott, Foresman, and Co., 3rd ed., 1964), pp. 108–113.

PART II. *THE SOCIAL FUNCTION OF LOVE* (pages 37–99)

1. See Adriano Tilgher, "Work Through the Ages," in Sigmund Nosow and William H. Form, eds., *Man, Work, and Society* (New York: Basic Books, 1962), pp. 11–14.

2. Morton M. Hunt, *The Natural History of Love*, p. 131.

3. See Nicholas J. Demerath and Richard A. Peterson, eds., *System, Change, and Conflict: A Reader on Contemporary Sociology and the Debate over Functionalism* (New York: The Free Press, 1967).

4. Talcott Parsons, "Durkheim's Contribution to the Theory of Integration of Social Systems," in Emile Durkheim et al., *Essays on Sociology and Philosophy*, ed. Kurt H. Wolff (New York: Harper Torchbooks, 1964), p. 119.

5. Thomas Hobbes, *Leviathan*, Part I, Chapter 13.

6. Emile Durkheim, *The Division of Labor in Society*, tr. George Simpson (New York: The Macmillan Co., 1933), pp. 79–80.

7. Durkheim, *The Elementary Forms of the Religious Life*, tr. Joseph Ward Swain (New York: The Free Press, 1965). See especially pp. 462 ff.

8. A. R. Radcliffe-Brown, *Structure and Function in Primitive Society* (New York: The Macmillan Co., 1965), p. 200.

9. See Robert K. Merton, *On Theoretical Sociology* (New York: The Free Press, 1967), Chapter 3, "Manifest and Latent Functions."

10. See Kingsley Davis, "The Myth of Functional Analysis as a Special Method in Sociology and Anthropology," *American Sociological Review*, 24 (Dec., 1959), pp. 752–772.

11. David Hume, *An Inquiry Concerning Human Understanding* (New York: The Liberal Arts Press, 1955), p. 52.

12. Durkheim, *The Elementary Forms*, p. 470.

13. See Edward Shorter, *The Making of the Modern Family* (New York: Basic Books, 1977), pp. 5–6.

14. Hunt, *The Natural History*, pp. 363–367.

15. In the sense used by Erving Goffman, *Frame Analysis: An Essay on the Organization of Experience* (New York: Harper and Row, 1974).

16. John H. Scanzoni, *Opportunity and the Family* (New York: The Free Press, 1970), p. 26.

17. Robert O. Blood, *Love Match and Arranged Marriage* (New York: The Free Press, 1967), p. 71.

18. Ezra Vogel, *Japan's New Middle Class* (Berkeley: University of California Press, 1963), p. 102.

19. Durkheim, *The Elementary Forms*, p. 56.

20. Goffman, *Interaction Ritual*, p. 53.

21. *Interaction Ritual*, p. 54.

22. *Interaction Ritual*, p. 85.

23. *Interaction Ritual*, p. 86.

24. *Interaction Ritual*, pp. 90–91.

25. Goffman, *Relations in Public: Microstudies of the Public Order* (New York: Basic Books, 1971), p. 373.

26. Hunt, *The Natural History*, pp. 131–172.

27. Philippe Ariès, *Centuries of Childhood: A Social History of Family Life*, tr. Robert Baldick (New York: Random House, 1962), pp. 355–356.

28. *Centuries of Childhood*, pp. 365–404.

29. Hunt, *The Natural History*, pp. 204–211.

30. Talcott Parsons and Neil J. Smelser, *Economy and Society*, (Glencoe, Ill.: The Free Press, 1956), p. 222.

31. This discussion is indebted to Talcott Persons, "The Normal American Family," in Marvin B. Sussman, ed., *Sourcebook in Marriage and the Family* (Boston: Houghton Mifflin Co., 3rd ed., 1968), pp. 36–46.

32. Ariès, *Centuries of Childhood*, p. 406.

33. Ralph Linton, "The Natural History of the Family," in Ruth Nanda Anshen, ed., *The Family: Its Function and Destiny* (New York: Harper and Bros., rev. ed., 1959), p. 46.

34. Ludwig Wittgenstein, *Philosophical Investigations*, Part II, Sect. iv.

35. George A. Theodorson, "Romanticism and Motivation to Marry in the United States, Singapore, Burma, and India," *Social Forces*, 44 (Sept., 1965), pp. 17–27.

36. Linton, "The Natural History of the Family," p. 52.

37. See George S. Rosenberg and Donald F. Anspach, *Working Class Kinship* (Lexington, Mass.: D. C. Heath and Co., 1973).

38. See Merton, *On Theoretical Sociology*.

39. Peter L. Berger and Thomas Luckmann, *The Social Construction of Reality: A Treatise in the Sociology of Knowledge* (Garden City, N.Y.: Anchor Books, 1967), pp. 129–163.

40. Goffman uses this list on p. 277 of *Frame Analysis*.

41. Parsons, "The Normal American Family," p. 39.

42. See Demerath and Peterson, *Systems, Change, and Conflict*; also Carl G. Hempel, *Aspects of Scientific Explanation and Other Essays in the Philosophy of Science* (New York: The Free Press, 1965), p. 319.

43. Erving Goffman, *Stigma: Notes on the Management of Spoiled Identity* (Englewood Cliffs, N.J.: Prentice-Hall, 1963), pp. 138–139.

44. Herbert Gans, "The Positive Functions of Poverty," *American Journal of Sociology*, 78 (1972), pp. 275–289.

45. Goffman, *Stigma*, p. 2.

46. Erving Goffman, *Encounters: Two Studies in the Sociology of Interaction* (Indianapolis: Bobbs-Merrill, 1961), p. 133.

47. M. Dorothy George, *London Life in the Eighteenth Century* (New York: Capricorn Books, 1965), p. 113.

PART III. INQUIRY AND THE INQUIRER (pages 101–143)

1. Bertrand Russell, *Mysticism and Logic and Other Essays* (Harmondsworth, Middlesex: Penguin Books, 1953), p. 46.

2. Aristotle, *Nicomachean Ethics*, I, 2, 1094a27–b10 (tr. W. D. Ross).

3. Spinoza, *Theologico-Political Treatise*, Chap. XIII, in *The Chief Works of*

Benedict de Spinoza, tr. R. H. M. Elwes, vol. I (New York: Dover, 1951), p. 177. See also: Harry A. Wolfson, *The Philosophy of Spinoza*, vol. I (New York: Meridian Books, 1958), pp. 144–145. *The Interpreter's Dictionary of the Bible* (New York and Nashville: Abingdon Press, 1962), s.v. "God, Names of" (esp. section B), "Jehovah."

4. Goffman, *Encounters*, p. 9.

5. See, for example, Aristotle, *Metaphysics*, II, 1, 993b21.

6. Charles Coulston Gillispie, *The Edge of Objectivity* (Princeton: Princeton University Press, 1960), p. 43.

7. See, for example, Jeffrey Burton Russell, *Witchcraft in the Middle Ages* (Ithaca, N.Y.: Cornell University Press, 1972), pp. 7–13.

8. Peter L. Berger, *The Sacred Canopy: Elements of a Sociological Theory of Religion* (Garden City, N.Y.: Doubleday and Co., Anchor Books ed., 1969), pp. 11–12.

9. See Thomas Luckmann, *The Invisible Religion: The Problem of Religion in Modern Society* (New York: Macmillan Publishing Co., Inc., 1967).

10. See Rem B. Edwards, *Reason and Religion: An Introduction to the Philosophy of Religion* (New York: Harcourt, Brace, Jovanovich, 1972).

11. *Reason and Religion*, p. 7.

12. "Compel them to come in" (Luke 14:23). For the significance of this text, see Henry Kamen, *The Rise of Toleration* (New York and Toronto: McGraw-Hill Book Co., 1967), pp. 236–237.

13. Berger, *The Sacred Canopy*, p. v.

14. Immanuel Kant, *Foundations of the Metaphysics of Morals*, Third Section; from *Critique of Practical Reason*, tr. Beck, p. 103.

15. Kant, *Critique of Pure Reason*, ed. Norman K. Smith (New York: St. Martin's Press, 1970), A iii.

Index